Superb translations says DONALD KEENE, America's most honored critic of Japanese literature, in his appreciation of this new work by the award winning translator, Robert Epp.

Maruyama Kaoru was for much of his life cut off from the Tokyo literary establishment both by distance and his refusal to conform to its dominant aesthetic - - intuitive lyricism. He drew his inspiration from early years at sea and later years teaching young children in an isolated mountain village in the Japanese Snow Country.

Japanese names are given in the traditional order, family name first.

Asian Poetry in Translation: Japan
Editor, Thomas Fitzsimmons

#1 *Devil's Wind: A Thousand Steps* by Yoshimasu Gôzô

#2 *Sun, Sand and Wind* by Shôzu Ben

#3 *A String Around Autumn: Selected Poems 1952-1980* by Ōoka Makoto

#4 *Treelike: The Poetry of Kinoshita Yûji*
 -- UNESCO Collection of Representative Works
 -- Japan-US Friendship Commission Translation Prize

#5 *Dead Languages: Selected Poems 1946-1984* by Tamura Ryûichi

#6 *Celebration in Darkness: Selected Poems of Yoshioka Minoru*
 &
 Strangers' Sky: Selected Poems of Iijima Kôichi

#7 *A Play of Mirrors: Eight Major Poets of Modern Japan*

#8 *A Thousand Steps . . . and More: Selected Poems and Prose 1964-1984* by Yoshimasu Gôzô

#9 *Demented Flute: Selected Poems 1967-1986* by Sasaki Mikirô

#10 *I Am Alive: The Tanka Poems* of Gotô Miyoko

#11 *Moonstone Woman: Selected Poems and Prose* by Tada Chimako

#12 *Self-Righting Lamp: Selected Poems* by Maruyama Kaoru

Supported by the National Endowment for the Arts, the Japan-US Friendship Commission, Oakland University (MI), University of Michigan Center for Japanese Studies, the Saison Cultural Foundation (Japan) and UNESCO.

Self-Righting Lamp
Selected Poems

UNESCO COLLECTION OF REPRESENTATIVE WORKS
JAPANESE SERIES

This work has been accepted by the Japanese National Commision for UNESCO as a representitive work of modern Japanese Literature

Asian Poetry in Translation : Japan #12

Self-Righting Lamp
Selected Poems

Maruyama Kaoru

Translated by
Robert Epp

Preface by Donald Keene

Katydid Books
Oakland University   Michigan

Copyright © 1990 by Katydid Books
English translations Copyright © 1990 by Robert Epp
Preface Copyright © 1990 by Donald Keene
Cover art Copyright © 1990 by Karen Hargreaves-Fitzsimmons

All rights reserved

First Edition

Produced by KT DID Productions, Inc
Printed in the United States of America
by Thomson-Shore, Dexter, MI

This book is printed on acid-free paper and its binding materials have been chosen for strength and durability.

KATYDID BOOKS:
K.H.-Fitzsimmons and T. Fitzsimmons, assisted by G.L. Robinson
c/o Department of English, Oakland University, Rochester, MI 48309-4401
FAX 313-370-2286

Library of Congress Cataloging in Publication Data

Maruyama, Kaoru, 1899 - 1974
    [Poems. English. Selections. 1990]
    Self-righting lamp : selected poems / Maruyama Kaoru ; translated by Robert Epp.
      p. cm. - - (Asian poetry in translation. Japan ; #12)
    ISBN 0-942668. - - ISBN 0-942668-24-3 (pbk.)
    1. Maruyama, Kaoru, 1899-1974- -Translations, English. I. Epp, Robert. II. Title. III. Series.
PL833.A7A6   1990
895.6'142 - - dc20   90-41265
                                                        CIP

TABLE OF CONTENTS

INTRODUCTORY

Foreword by Donald Keene 13
Translator's Introduction 17
Acknowledgements 32

THE POETRY

Part One: (1926–1947) 33
Part Two: (1948–1974) 69

SUPPLEMENTARY

Notes on the Poems 109
Data on the Collections 117
English Titles 119

These translations are for

TAMESADA NOBUYUKI and his late wife YUKIKO

FOREWORD
Donald Keene

In the past, when Japanese interested in translating their country's literature into English have asked me what works would be appropriate, I have generally suggested that they try modern poetry. It has been my experience that the greatest difficulty for a person who translates into a language that is not his native one is the special rhythms of prose. Again, minor lapses in grammar or peculiar usage that would be glaringly conspicuous in a prose translation can sometimes, by their unfamiliarity, even enhance lines of poetry; nobody expects that poetry will observe the same rules as prose. I am not sure if anyone has actually taken my advice. I hope not. Robert Epp's superb translations of the poetry of Maruyama Kaoru have made me realize how irresponsible my suggestion was.

It is indeed possible to translate poetry into something that resembles poetry even if one is not completely fluent in the language into which the translation is made. The imagery and sometimes the thought pervading the original poem may be so compelling that it will survive the translation of the rankest amateur. Only when one compares such translations with those made by a poet in his own right does one understand how much can be lost by a "literal" translation.

Robert Epp's translations of Maruyama date back at least to 1972 when he published a selection in the *Beloit Poetry Journal*. I remember reading them at the time and being favorably impressed. But, not satisfied with these entirely competent versions, which other translators would have been happy to acknowledge as their own, he has painstakingly gone over each translation again and again, in the effort to be as faithful as possible both to the meaning of the originals and to their specifically poetic qualities. A comparison of his earlier and newer versions of almost any poem will illustrate the nature of the changes he has made. Here is the 1972 version of "Song of the Sail":

> Gull wings beat the dark sky of the sea;
>   if I dip my shoulders
>   I think I might touch them.
> Gull cries shriek the dark sky of the sea;
>   if I reach out my hands
>   I think I might catch them.
> I could capture them
>   but for the flickering lamp
> that dangles from my neck.
>   I'll blow it out and wait for the gull
> to come and light upon
> the snuffed–out blackness of the flame.

The revised version is:

> Gull wings beating in the sea's dark skies;
>   dipping my shoulder maybe I could touch them
> Gull cries mewing in the sea's dark skies;
>   if I reach out maybe I could catch them.
> But flickers from the lamp hanging from my neck
>   keep the gull from seeing me.
> I'll blow the lamp out
> then wait for the gull to come and perch
>   on the cold lamp's sooted wick.

I chose this particular poem as an illustration because I had much admired it even in its earlier state. The new version does not change the meaning in any way -- this is not a case of a translator who has had second thoughts about the accuracy of his version -- but tightens and makes more effective the poetic expression by eliminating words that are unnecessary in English and therefore tend to dilute the intensity. "If I reach out my hands" became "reaching out." Needless to say, even the earlier version was not batted out automatically on a typewriter while glancing at the original text; the poet in Robert Epp controlled that translation, too, though not quite so masterfully as in his new version. The line in question reads in Japanese: "*te wo nobaseba te ni tsukame–sô da.*" A more literal translation, of the kind that many translators might make, would be, "If I stretch out my hands it seems as if I could catch them in my hands." It would be hard to explain to anyone who knows only words and has no ear for the English language what is wrong with this version; it is accurate but a betrayal of the original. I shudder to think of the translations of modern Japanese poetry that may have been made in keeping with my misguided suggestion.

The poems in *Self-Righting Lamp* are the product of the infiltration, over a long period of time, of the works of a major Japanese poet into the mind and spirit of an American translator. Maruyama Kaoru is not a household name even in Japan. His poetry, though in no way forbidding, lacks the familiar touch that is likely to endear a poet to his countrymen. The poems are filled instead with the loneliness of a poet who seemed happier when surrounded by the vastness of the ocean than when caught up in the concerns of modern society.

Maruyama was by no means indifferent to other people. His sympathies were naturally with those, like himself, who had known the sting of failure and neglect. Many poems are moving especially because of their empathy with people and things that would be totally forgotten if they did not stubbornly linger in the poet's memory. Perhaps this nostalgia is what first attracted Epp to Maruyama and induced him later to revise his versions of the poems. Each change that he has made in his translations surely reflects hours of beating out the rhythms and trying to capture the music of the originals in English. The translations not only do justice to Maruyama Kaoru and make him accessible to the English–reading world but are themselves enjoyable for their beauty as English poems.

INTRODUCTION

The contemporary poet–critic Ooka Makoto writes that "in modern Japan it has sometimes been disastrous to be called an 'intellectual poet.'" Japanese regard intellect, Ooka says, as an "obstruction, intrusive and suspect."

It is a very short distance from that attitude to actually cherishing the irrational elements implicit in intuitive creativity. If a poet self–consciously uses intellect as a means of shaping, controlling, or moderating feelings, he or she may find it difficult to achieve wide–spread or lasting popularity in Japan. This may explain why so few Japanese presently read the verse of Maruyama Kaoru (1899–1974). His consistent attempt to keep his lyrical impulse and sentimentality under the control of his reason makes him "suspect." Readers in Japan prefer to feel intuitively involved in the poet's innermost life. When they cannot do this, Japanese will not read the poet.

Because he has written much excellent poetry, it becomes somewhat difficult for the average critic simply to dismiss Maruyama out of hand. The difficulty encourages subconscious stratagems. The reader can, for example, neatly avoid dealing with the poet's cerebral aspects and react only to what he might subjectively perceive in the poetry as "interesting," more congenial to his expectations and taste, or easier to deal with. Utilizing this particular maneuver, critics in Japan like to play up and concentrate on Maruyama's interest in the sea. The nearly universal tendency in Japan to label Maruyama "the poet of the sea" effectively distances the reader from his often self–conscious intellectuality.

Describing Maruyama's work in this limited way effectively negates his achievements, his artistic growth, and the actual range of his concerns.

Even commentators who praise the imagistic aspects of Maruyama's verse ignore or give short shrift to qualities that give his work greater depth than the "sea–poet" label suggests. The tag, moreover, allows critics to ignore some eighty percent of Maruyama's production and most of his cherished concerns. Small wonder that during interviews the poet frequently expressed great displeasure over such pigeon–holing.

No one, of course, wants to deny that an important part of Maruyama's output has something to do with the sea. The titles of three of his fifteen collections relate to the sea. But a close look at the poems themselves makes it difficult to claim that most works in these three books exemplify a "love for the sea." And when we consider a representative cross–section of Maruyama's entire output, we certainly do not find a poet committed to writing paeans to the sea, any more than we find a poet primarily concerned with feelings. We discover a writer dealing with perception, isolation, illusions, human relations, and the like, a poet whose quest is essentially intellectual. He seeks the whole self, identity, a meaning for life, the ways that an individual might relate to others and to his innermost being. The sea serves Maruyama as a powerful metaphor of the psyche he wishes to understand so as to achieve an inner harmony that can be "self–righting."

Maruyama's sense of being a "loner" called for such harmony. He spent most of his life physically removed from Tokyo poetry circles. This probably intensified a sense of isolation resulting from certain childhood experiences. The central government transferred his father, a high–ranking bureaucrat, frequently enough so that the poet's boyhood seemed to consist of constant uprooting and the constant need to make new friends. By the time he was twelve, Maruyama had attended four different primary schools; he transferred to the fifth school soon after his father died. In Japan's tightly–knit society, particularly in the milieu of Maruyama's boyhood, families would only rarely move from one location to another. That made it very difficult for the new boy in class to make friends and become accepted. Maruyama consequently suffered from isolation. A frail constitution that often kept him out of school increased his sense of separateness; during bouts of high fever, the feeling that he did not belong helped generate nightmares.

These experiences ultimately nurtured in Maruyama the dream of becoming a ship's captain. In 1911 he went with his elementary school class to the port of Yokohama to see a flying machine demonstration. Rain forced cancellation of the flight, so the teacher took his class to look at ships in the harbor. There the blue eyes of some Scandinavian sailors astonished the young Maruyama. He dates his focus on the sea from that experience. Consequently, after graduating from middle school six years later, Maruyama sat -- despite strong opposition from his mother and relatives -- for the entrance examination to the Merchant Marine Academy. He could make his own decisions in such matters because he was, after all, the *pro forma* family head. He failed the examination but promptly enrolled in a Tokyo preparatory school, intending to retake the test the following year. In April 1918 Maruyama passed the exam and entered the Academy.

From the outset Maruyama had hoped to become master of his own ship. He soon discovered, however, that his fear of heights made it impossible to climb the masts, which meant he could not qualify as a line officer. That left the engine room; but an engineer could never become a ship's captain. The dream, then, was over. Furthermore, the intense physical activity required of trainees caused his legs to swell enough to incapacitate him, so he received a medical release in September 1918. Still obsessed by unsatisfied longings to experience the sea, he briefly considered becoming a lighthouse keeper. His mother managed to persuade him to take the examination for the Third Higher School in Kyoto, a major route to the elite University of Tokyo. After careful preparation, he passed the test and matriculated in 1921 as a French literature major. His choice of majors reflected both his hope to become a writer, perhaps a journalist, and his deep aversion to becoming a bureaucrat.

Through his reading of modern Japanese poets, French poetry in translation, and works by Edgar Allen Poe and Oscar Wilde, Maruyama soon found a new goal -- poetry. His fresh interest encouraged him to pay very little attention to the curriculum. He in fact missed so many classes in Kyoto that he ended up repeating two years. This delayed his graduation until March 1926.

By the time Maruyama entered Tokyo University in April 1926 as a Japanese literature major, he had decided to become a poet. Because he did not consider working except as a poet, which in prewar days meant a life of abject poverty, he did not need a bachelor's degree. He sought instead all the literary stimulation the campus promised. The university indeed provided the perfect environment to realize this dream. It allowed Maruyama to associate with many would–be poets, discuss Japanese and European poetry, and help edit a literary magazine in which he might publish his writings. He thought he could afford to devote himself exclusively to poetry because he imagined that his father's inheritance would allow him quite a few years of financial independence.

Nearly total involvement in poetry and writing did not prevent Maruyama from associating with those less committed than he to literary endeavors. One such friend at Tokyo University, whom he knew from the Third Higher School in Kyoto, lived in Toyohashi. Going home with him on vacation, Maruyama met Takai Miyoko (b. 1907), the daughter of a draper. Spinal caries had forced Miyoko to withdraw from the girls' school she had entered with the hope of becoming an English teacher. Maruyama's friendship with her bloomed during his frequent visits. Following their marriage in February 1928, he rented a luxurious residence in Tokyo (he had very expensive tastes) and six months later invited his mother to move in. Fortunately she got along well with Miyoko. Shortly afterward, the poet dropped out of school to concentrate on writing.

Economic hardships preceded the publication of his first book of poems. By 1930, the year of the financial crash in Japan, Maruyama had squandered the last of his father's inheritance. Over the ensuing months the penurious Maruyamas found themselves moving from one place to another. His poverty made it extremely difficult to concentrate on the writing he knew he must do, for he had not yet properly "launched" his career with a well-received first collection.

The situation improved dramatically in the autumn of 1931. Through a friend, the poet found Miyoko a job in downtown Tokyo. The couple promptly left Kyoto and settled in the capital. Until nearly the end of 1944, his wife's more than adequate income allowed Maruyama to concentrate on poetry. His first collection, *Sail-Lamp-Gull [Ho-Ranpu-Kamome]*, appeared in December 1932; he was thirty-three. The title refers to three poems that describe the ironic viewpoints of a sail, a lamp, and a gull. This trilogy examines in a single moment of time and space the difficulty of achieving relationship. The poetry's unique, concrete, and finely-honed imagery made quite a positive impact on Tokyo poetry circles.

Not long after issuing *Sail-Lamp-Gull,* Maruyama decided to join others in publishing *Shiki [Four Seasons].* This decision affected his entire career. Maruyama's connection with the magazine and with those who edited and contributed to it kept him involved in Tokyo poetry circles even though he lived far from the capital, and even when *Shiki* was not being published. Association with the journal also vitally contributed to the development of Maruyama's aesthetic.

He derived his poetic from a number of sources, three of which are particularly worth noting. Hori Tatsuo (1904–1953) surely influenced him. During student days at Tokyo University, Hori translated several modern French poets and familiarized himself with contemporary European literary theory. Committed to a psychological approach to writing, his prescription for modern literature stressed balancing intellectuality with lyrical sensitivity. This attitude closely parallels the views of Hagiwara Sakutarô (1886–1942), the poet Maruyama most respected. Hagiwara had written about his approach to poetry in *The Principles of Poetry [Shiron]* (1928) and later joined those putting out *Shiki*.

Finally, the ideas of Ranier Maria Rilke (1875–1926) influenced Maruyama through both Hori and other *Shiki* writers. Rilke wrote of the need to use one's sensibilities to articulate the intellect. He talked of uncovering forgotten psychological truths about the mind. He had strong symbolist tendencies, too, and a penchant for personifying abstractions. He struggled constantly to be objective. All these qualities agree with Maruyama's aesthetic. At the very least, the poetic principles that he eventually forged for himself reflect the ideas that Rilke, Hagiwara, and Hori espoused.

The basis of Maruyama's aesthetic is his attempt to harmonize sentiment and intellect. His concept of "intellectual lyricism" aims not only to reconcile mind and feelings, but to suggest the process by which a poem comes to life. When an objective idea and a subjective image coalesce, Maruyama claims, you have the seed of a poem. This concept signifies Maruyama's desire to strike a balance between ideas and feelings. Thus the key to Maruyama's poetic grammar is lyricism tempered by intellect: a technique through which he hoped to control the indigenous penchant for indulging in purely lyrical or subjective feelings.

This, he thought, would result in poetry that has two characteristics. Not only would it affect the reader more powerfully than merely lyrical or sentimental verse, it would also increase the work's lyrical distance and so reduce the chance of inadvertently producing bathos. While not lacking in sentiment, such verse would be "cool" and "dry" enough to transcend sentimentality. Among other results, an increase in rationality would also make it easier for the poet to produce uniform results.

Maruyama's production since the early 1930s demonstrates how he has pursued this aesthetic. His artistic objectives have made his work demonstrably unique even among fellow *Shiki* poets. Certainly he may be celebrated for his profound existential awareness, one that seldom allows him to revel in atmosphere or image for their own sakes. Systematically applying such principles to his work, Maruyama continued to expand his reputation. In 1935 he published two books: *Funeral of the Crane [Tsuru no Sôshiki]* (May) and *Infancy [Yônen]* (June). The latter contains works that date from college days. He himself termed this verse a "bit sentimental" after it had won the initial prize conferred by the *Bungei Hanron* poetry magazine. More important than the prize money, the award brought Maruyama publicity and requests for manuscripts.

A short time before learning that *Infancy* had won the *Hanron* Prize, Maruyama's sister–in–law Kunié came down with consumption. Following graduation from girls' school in Toyohashi, Kunié had in April 1932 moved to Tokyo to live with the Maruyamas; she found employment with the same firm as Miyoko. Kunié returned home in January 1936 and died in March. She was only twenty–four. The poet's friendship with Kunié antedated by several years his acquaintance with Miyoko. His admiring sister–in–law had been close to him, so her death affected him profoundly.

His fourth collection, *A Single Day [Ichinichishû]* (1936), contains an entire section of poems about Kunié's death. These works stand less as monuments to her memory than as records of how Maruyama tried as an artist to deal with her loss. The fact that he published several more Kunié poems five years later in his fifth collection may suggest how long it took him to expunge his grief.

In certain particulars, works dealing with Kunić's death both resemble and differ from those in the earlier collections. One significant resemblance lies in the persona's attitude toward the effectiveness of poetry to communicate his feelings. Maruyama laments the inadequacy of mere words to express his deep anguish, protesting that he can neither deal verbally with his tragedy nor address God about it.

A major difference is that -- unlike most verse in *Sail–Lamp–Gull*, for instance -- poems dealing with Kunié's death derive from deep–felt experience. They have not issued from abstract hopes and dreams, or from the poet's failure to realize them. As direct expressions of actual experience, these poems give us the sense that the poet has demonstrated virtually for the first time a willingness to share his private emotions. This contrasts notably with earlier descriptions of his feelings. In many if not most earlier works, he so objectifies the described emotions, and so effectively keeps his sentiments under control, that we remain relatively distant observers of his emotions. The Kunié poems illustrate at least a willingness to involve the reader directly in the poet's grief. Conscious control of the impulses fueling these works keeps Maruyama from losing the lyrical distance that makes the poems work.

Several months after issuing his fifth collection, *Concrete Images [Busshô Shishû]* (February 1941), Maruyama finally realized his boyhood dream of going to sea. *The Central Review [Chûô Kôron]*, an important intellectual journal, had appointed him a special correspondent assigned the task of depicting the midshipmen's experiences at sea. He left May 4 aboard the *Neptune [Kaiô Maru]*, a four–masted naval training barque. In July Maruyama began turning his notes and journalistic accounts into poetry. It took him several years to get this book in order. As he worked up his sea poems, he published his sixth collection, *The God Who Wept [Namida Shita Kami]* (February 1942), which contains only nine new selections, none related to his cruise on the *Neptune*. His sea poems finally appeared in September 1943 titled, *Hear the Ship's Bell [Tenshô naru Tokoro]* (literally, "where the ship's bell sounds").

On the most superficial level, the thirty–four works in this collection constitute an informative and fascinating record of life aboard an old–time sailing vessel. On another level, they exhibit a style far more open and far less symbolic than anything seen in Maruyama's earlier work. For one thing, this verse has an immediacy similar to that noted in the poems written about Kunié's death. These poems are far less intense, of course, but they similarly grow out of concrete experiences, not from reading or dreaming about the sea. Moreover, Maruyama clearly intends these works for a more general audience. Dense compression and lyric distancing, so characteristic of Maruyama's pre–1940 attempts to maintain control of his feelings, become rare.

None of this should be taken to mean that the verses in *Hear the Ship's Bell* are merely vacuous odes to the sea or simple–minded ethnographic descriptions of life aboard a sailing vessel. True, these poems contain considerably more every–day language and relaxed imagery than we can find in earlier verse. But Maruyama by no means reacts only on the superficial level to his feelings or experiences aboard ship. Nor do his basic concerns with issues like perspective reversal, illusions of time and space, or the ever–present problem of keeping himself from being "off plumb," the need for personal stability, change in the least. He remains the poet he was. He simply begins to use more relaxed language.

Meanwhile, national efforts to survive the war became considerably more intense. Within a year and a half after Maruyama returned from his voyage on the *Neptune*, Japan had begun to experience the ravages of war directly. By the winter of 1945, in fact, the Pacific conflict had begun to touch the lives of the common people in practically every major city. Only Kyoto escaped visits from American bombers. Consumer goods had nearly disappeared from department stores. Fire bombings had forced people to desert the metropolitan areas in droves. Shortages of merchandise in the Tokyo department stores forced the company Miyoko worked for, and which she had been managing for some years, out of business.

Creating poetry in such an environment was virtually impossible. Consequently, when the opportunity arose to teach elementary school in Iwanezawa, Yamagata Prefecture, a remote hamlet in the mountains of northern Honshu and far removed from fire bombs, Maruyama decided to take it. He headed north in early spring and began teaching in April 1945.

Maruyama's escape to the "snow country" must certainly have seemed to him like starting life afresh. This was, after all, the first time he had had a steady job of any kind. Childless, this was the first time he had to communicate with small children. It was also the first time Maruyama had lived so many months separated from wife, family, friends, and literary colleagues. To make this experience all the more poignant, a B–29 raid in May reduced his Tokyo home in Nakano to ashes. The Maruyamas lost practically all their possessions, and Miyoko no longer had a roof over her head. The news of this loss so upset the poet that he precipitously deserted Iwanezawa and, hoping to locate Miyoko, headed directly for Tokyo. Accompanied by his mother and wife, he returned to his teaching post early in September.

Actually, life in the mountains seemed much more than a fresh beginning. Absolutely every experience stimulated his imagination. Everything was totally new to him, including the local brogue he sometimes had difficulty understanding. Unlike Miyoko, he never tried to speak anything but the standard language of Tokyo. The newness inspired him tremendously. Never had Maruyama written so feverishly as during those years in the north. Virtually overwhelmed by inspiration and, subsequently, by requests for manuscripts, he produced a steadily increasing stream of verse.

These busy times provided the Maruyamas with the opportunity to consolidate themselves financially. More important than several years of building up his bank account, days in the north allowed -- or, more precisely, they required -- the poet to grow as a human being and as an artist. He learned ever more effectively how the creation of poetry functioned like a self-righting lamp on his psyche. With ample opportunity to reflect, observe, study, and hone his skills, these years gave him new perspectives on life and art, experiences he constantly stressed during interviews.

Of course, Maruyama had to expend considerable energies adjusting to the harsh environment and to the hardy northern people he grew to admire. A man accustomed to living in spacious, well-appointed Western surroundings could only with conscious effort adjust to living in a single, sparsely furnished Japanese-style room. The discipline required was certainly an important factor in helping give the poet a fresh perspective on life. His efforts to adapt bore fruit, too, as in the end he became a stronger person and a more versatile poet. He confessed that the process of adjusting to existence in the mountains permanently altered the way he viewed himself and others. He felt that experiences in Iwanezawa, having enriched and leavened both his poetry and his life, allowed him to develop dynamically as an artist and a man. The years he spent there were literally lessons in becoming human.

These lessons naturally affected his poetry. In terms of content, after his brief snow country interlude Maruyama's poetry shows an increasing range of interests and concerns. He found it easier to write about personal and general human problems that he had hesitated to deal with before 1945 -- unless he treated the material in an oblique or symbolic manner. In terms of method, his postwar work displays a consistently direct and relaxed nature, at least on the surface. By then, he could more effectively communicate his poetic insights to the average poetry lover, a fact evidenced by the steadily increasing number of requests for poems from editors of non-intellectual and non-specialist magazines and journals. Apparently, Maruyama had mastered new ways to order his materials, to maintain appropriate artistic distance from his emotions, and to clothe his experience in simple and direct language. Throughout this process of maturation, conscious artistry continues to maintain intellectual control of his work.

Two of the three collections inspired by life in Iwanezawa deal with the local people, customs, and landscapes. The third reflects Maruyama's experiences with the school children. Few of these pieces treat directly the poet's personal problems or artistic concerns. Nevertheless, the north country poems clearly indicate that it would be a mistake to assume that Maruyama had surrendered or compromised his aesthetic simply because he had temporarily moved into the snow country. Much verse written in the north depicts the poet's observations of life in a radically new environment. Ostensibly, these works resemble Maruyama's depictions of experiences on his two voyages at sea. The snow that for half the year so deeply buries almost everything visible to the eye no doubt reminded him of the vast covering power of the sea.

Iwanezawa's remoteness guaranteed that it would be safe from the B–29. This, of course, allowed Maruyama many worry-free hours to devote himself to poetry. He was by no means safe, however, from gnawing doubts about his future as a poet. The more he wrote, the more requests he received for manuscripts. The more these requests motivated him to be productive, the more of a nuisance teaching little children became and the more he longed for the stimulation of fellow intellectuals in the capital.

Unfortunately, Tokyo suffered from shortages of housing, food, and jobs, not to mention run-away inflation as well as severely damaged transportation and distribution systems. Officials consequently discouraged people from returning to the capital unless they had gainful employment and a domicile. Maruyama of course had neither. At least, he figured, he could immerse himself in writing, so he resigned his teaching post as of March 1947, the end of the Japanese school year.

Although he continued to hope that he might soon be able to return to Tokyo, he decided to sit out the reconstruction of the capital and write poetry in the north. He remained in Iwanezawa another eighteen months. During that time, Maruyama published furiously. He issued three books in 1948: his ninth collection, *The Magical Country [Senkyô]* (March), his tenth, a book of children's poems, *The Blue Chalkboard [Aoi Kokuban]*

(May), and his eleventh, *Flowercore [Hana no Shin]* (June). Yet he knew that for the sake of his future as a poet he had to return to Tokyo. He had mined the experiences of the classroom and the snow country. It was time to move on.

Government authorities, however, continued to discourage people from returning to the shortage-ridden capital. That left Maruyama with no choice if he wanted to leave the north country. He must go to where he had roots, to Miyoko's hometown. So he left Iwanezawa in 1948 and settled down in Toyohashi to write. Although he fully intended to return to Tokyo as soon as feasible, Maruyama became ever more firmly rooted in Toyohashi. For example, in April 1949 he agreed to become a lecturer on modern Japanese poetry at Aichi University, a local private institution that eventually made him a visiting professor of literature. In the end, plans to return to the capital having failed, the poet increasingly regarded himself a "lone wolf."

Going on fifty when he moved to Toyohashi, Maruyama had a good deal of poetry left in him. Several years after his fiftieth birthday he published his twelfth collection, *Lost Youth [Seishun Fuzai]* (1952). He waited an entire decade before issuing his thirteenth book, *The Hostage Sea [Tsuresarareta Umi]*, whose title poem grieves over the way increasing pollution had taken the ocean hostage. Maruyama based all new poems in this 1962 work on his 1955 cruise to Australia aboard the freighter *Yamashita Maru*. To circumvent government restrictions against civilian travel abroad, the poet had been officially listed as the ship's purser.

It took him several years to shape these experiences at sea into satisfactory verse. Health crises account in part for the delay in publication. In 1956, he had two-thirds of an ulcerated stomach removed; in 1958, a problem with intestinal blockage required major surgery. But he apparently also encountered difficulties similar to those experienced when he attempted to convert into poetry his notes from the 1943 *Neptune* voyage.

Following another ten-year hiatus, he published in 1972 the next collection, *Moon Passage [Tsuki Wataru]*, his fourteenth. He issued his fifteenth and last book, *Face with Ants [Ari no iru Kao]*, a year later. These two works contain a number of poems that fully support Maruyama's claim to significant artistic development since leaving Tokyo early in 1945 for Iwanezawa. He manages to imply in these poems considerably more than in most earlier verse, partly through skillful juxtapositions of imagery and symbols. Throughout, he mixes poignant but relaxed diction and common experience with uncommon symbolism and suggestion. In this way, he achieves in aggregate far greater depth and range than in the majority of his earlier work.

The verbal surfaces of most poems in the first collection, *Sail–Lamp–Gull*, are complex, the symbolic and metaphorical structures relatively uncomplicated. As one might expect as a result of experience and maturity, the surface texture of his last published poetry is fairly simple and direct, the symbolic organization quite elaborate. In his earliest poetry Maruyama examines, as he did in the sail–lamp–gull trilogy, the elementary notions of relatedness and isolation. He continues to deal with similar ideas in later works, but with greater profundity. His works also deal with far more intricate interrelationships, multiple meanings, and extremely involved issues that, almost without exception, contain general significance.

Hardening of the arteries made it increasingly difficult for Maruyama to be very active. After the spring of 1974, he spent part of each month in the Ogino Hospital in Toyokawa, a suburb of Toyohashi. There he received the personal ministrations of Doctor Ogino Akihisa, a dedicated Maruyama supporter, lover of literature, and writer of short stories. Despite Dr. Ogino's efforts, Maruyama died at home on 21 October 1974 of a cerebral thrombosis. He was seventy–five, his only heir his loving wife Miyoko.

Though he had spent many years out of the Tokyo main-stream,

Maruyama would still appear on almost any list of the dozen or so most important and representative modern Japanese poets. His poems consistently reveal an artist practicing his eye, sharpening his craft, and expanding his poetic -- which is to say his human -- range. Beyond that, the Iwanezawa phase of Maruyama's career very clearly demonstrates an independent-minded writer who consciously shed certain aspects of the elitism dominating poetry circles in the capital.

Life in the north vastly broadened his perspective and increased his ability to deal with and write for plain people. It also helped him stabilize his relationship with himself. All this occurred without compromising either his commitment to intellectual control of his art or his passion for symbolic statement. Experience out of the mainstream helped make Maruyama a poet for all readers.

To facilitate appreciation of Maruyama's development as an artist, I have arranged these works chronologically. My aim is to present a body of translations that will honestly reflect the range and depth of this poet's art. It is my hope that Maruyama would agree that the works translated below represent a genuine cross-section of his nearly fifty years of poetic activity.

An asterisk (*) after a poem title refers the reader to a note on that work (from page 107). A dot (•) after the final line on a page signifies a stanza break.

Acknowledgments

It is impossible to credit everyone who has contributed to these translations and to my study of Maruyama Kaoru. Any list, however, must begin with the late poet and his widow, Miyoko. They graciously responded to questions, extended hospitality, and otherwise put me deeply in their debt.

The poet also introduced me to Professor Nagata Masao, scholar of English literature, published poet, and translator of English verse. I have exploited his knowledge of Maruyama's poetry and accepted many suggestions for improving the accuracy and aptness of my translations. I am thankful, too, to Mr. Haraguchi Saburô of Toyohashi and Ms. Watanabe Hanako of Iwanezawa who have over the years responded to my countless annoying questions with patience and thoroughness.

I am profoundly grateful to Professors Iida Gakuji and Ben Befu for so often and so willingly untangling mysteries of syntax and meaning. The poet Thomas Fitzsimmons, as well as Doctors Elva Kremenliev and Donald Brannan, and Professors Arthur Kimball and Enno Klammer, suggested innumerable improvements in either the translations or the Introduction. I also appreciate Professor Donald Keene's taking time from a busy schedule to write the Foreword.

Finally, Mitsuko deserves thanks for endless re-typing and for help in preparing the title index.

Earlier versions of some poems appeared in the *American P.E.N. Review*, the *Hiram Poetry Review*, and *Poet Lore*. *The Beloit Poetry Journal* (Summer 1972) published nearly eighty of my translations of Maruyama, most of which appear below in different form. Four north country poems also appeared in the *Journal of Asian Culture* (XI, 1987).

POETRY PUBLISHED BETWEEN

1926 and 1947

Fabrications

A boy's fabrications
charged with sundry and singular dreams
have the adroitness of white-winged sea birds who stitch the waves
so only when Father and Mother were deceived
did his parents seem noble in the boy's eyes
But who can say he has no regrets?
When something too lovely wings in from afar
    and lodges in the lad's heart
as when flowers suddenly burst beautifully into bloom
or when twilight on sky's distant edges sparkles the world pink
who can say he never shed tears into skies into clouds
saying   The only one deceived was I?

The Fisherman

One day a fisherman's son
dreamt that his father shouldered the bronze-bowl sun
rolled up into his arms gorgeous sea-crowning clouds
and from beyond the dazzling sea
dashed toward him like an anchor

One night a fisherman's mother
dreamt that her son rode a shoal of sharks and the Black Current
trying to snare stars from dawn's fish-scale skies
darting away like a lightning flash
to some distant seashore lonely as a palace of ice

One morning a fisherman
dreamt his son's and mother's white hands
pulled open twilight's petalled clouds
then closed them like roses in the skies
over hometown shores beyond his sight

Infancy

I was born long ago in a lovely old spire under flitting bird shadows
hemmed in by sweets and maids
a blue–bearded marquis for a father
Sleeping in my cradle by that window framed with evening clouds
I remember having heard pensively in my dreams
someone singing lullabies of a far–off magical glen

I was born long ago in an isolated glen that soaked up even starlight
as I struggled day and night with deer or wolves
I hunted Mother through mountain tops boiling with mist
Dozing in my wind–rocked tree top cradle
I had the vague impression that I had mournfully heard
someone singing lullabies of that far–off magical spire

By Train

I'll take a train
to an Irish kind of countryside
I'll go to an Irish–like countryside
where rain streams through sunshine
and people twirl festive parasols
I'll cross lakes   thread tunnels
traveling with my face reflected on the window
I'll go to an Irish kind of countryside
where fine–faced girls and cattle roam

Views of the Harbor

Evening sunlight from China
shines on hotels on funnels on rickshas
on sailors' caps•

Wind from America
whips through masts through flags through smoke
through poplars by the road

Waves from the offing
ripple against launches against small boats against anchor chains
even against the red buoy by the jetty

From each and every scene
sailors' whistles pipe the sunset in.

Gun Emplacement*
Fragments yearned to snuggle together.
Fissures yearned to smile once more.
The mortar barrel yearned to rise and be seated again on its mount.
All were dreaming of transitory wholeness.
Each wind whip buried them deeper under sand.
The sea beyond sight ------ The flash of a migratory bird.

Song of the Sail
Gull wings beating in the sea's dark skies;
  dipping my shoulder maybe I could touch them.
Gull cries mewing in the sea's dark skies;
  if I reach out maybe I could catch them.
But flickers from the lamp hanging round my neck
  keep the gull from seeing me.
I'll blow the lamp out.
then wait for the gull to come and perch
  on the cold lamp's sooted wick.

Song of the Lamp
The anchor chain disappears into sea's dark depths
    beyond the reach of sight.
Rigging flees into the mast's dark heights beyond the reach of sight.
My feeble rays light only my sightless face.
Eyeing me the sea gull mews from the distant dark
    beyond where I can see.

Song of the Gull
I can't even see myself.
How much less could the lamp see me or the sail reflecting its light?
Yet lamp and sail are clearly visible from here
I just wheel through the distant frozen dark.

Funeral of the Crane
Finally at dusk a single cloud
    sunbeams swelling its eyes with tears
    sank behind the little hill in the yard
Apparently awaiting a breeze
    soon it lifted long–stiffened wings
    and stole away through the back gate
From the pine–covered slope I caught a brief
    chilled glance of it in the western sky
For some days since still no sign of rain

Mountain Pass
Nipped by grinding gears that gasp for breath
the locomotive whistles its warnings
When the engine scales the zigzag to the heights
a yellow lily behind the grade marker looking off after the train

contracts like a painful blink
beyond the tunnel's arch
and those pointed peaks looming ever nearer
exchange intimate greetings with sunset silhouettes
The dim lamp makes even my face by the window another shadow
rambling sadly over the distant slopes of the gorge

Day–Long Dreams
My studio washed by morning sun
I hastily take a carpenter's plane
to confront that rose–colored pillar
and scatter those scraps of dream threatening again to sparkle
    through my day

Song of the Spring Bird
Not even oats
will sprout from such barren soil
nor does the glow of one dandelion touch it
A bird wonders what those gravel lumps have in mind
Tentatively he claws at one breaking it up
and when he pecks at the obstinate core
sparks that sadden twilight scatter faintly into his eyes

Monk Hill
No pines grow on Monk Hill
no crags there
only the rustling of bamboo grass
Whichever direction you turn
rose winds pass over your chilled face and
as they give way to gathering sunbeams

skylarks fly up from under violets
Have the larks come back?
One got lost in the field
Presently when night's ring of stars begins to glisten
I hear the banter of water drops
like bells tinkling in one's breast

Afternoon
On a cloudy urban afternoon
crows scurry off
through the space over harried roof tops
through skies over the river where a whistle shrills
Footfalls instantly snarling with space
the crows' willowy receding figures
momentarily float into the telescope of my nostalgia
One speaks to the other with a shadowy voice
its partner's reply unheard

Perversity*
Ah I stretch out on this vast this dreary
this shadowless clump of chalky emptiness and
taking out my pocket mirror once again
today I gaze at it hard enough to plunge through it into my Self
into that far–off Self deep within eyes gazing at my Self

Bell Song
Living through the day with your photograph
I tinkle the little bell you loved
trying to call the soul in your picture back to life
Your likeness   startled   widely opens its eyes

and silently comes to lean on me
Ah soft black hair shedding light
wind lips whispering a thousand echoless words
I shake the bell harder   I shake it   I make it sing
but its thin string slips like a shriek from my finger
and ends up on a rock in my crane deserted yard

Self–Righting Lamp

    I love the lamps they lit on sea voyages in the old days. You know, those self–righting lamps that always returned to the vertical despite being swayed endlessly by waves.---- As a boy, I had often dreamed of becoming a sailor.

    Years later. The winds of this world tease the sails of life ---- nevertheless that lamp spinning under my ribs even now keeps the silent flame of my poetry perfectly plumb.

The God Who Wept[*]
The soldiers had done more than was human
Some of the wounded
had now returned to the land of their birth

I visited a friend
lying on a white pillow by a window
in the Second Army Hospital in Tokyo
He stared from between hospital gown and bandages
at winter sun fading on the wall

I reached out
intending to pat that close–cropped head
where once a god had dwelled
but the comely stubble prickled my palm•

Instantly his eyes filled with tears
"That tickles" he said smiling   and turned his head

Touching Your Tombstone
You told me before your lungs rotted and you died:
Take the lane by the graveyard in dusk's gloom!
Inexplicable warmths will dangle from your back
glints of butterflies and moths will prickle your cheeks
It only seems but isn't really eerie because
those ranked stones stand through the lengthy day
their stored warmths slow to cool

This evening I happened to be out strolling
and by chance passed the gate of this familiar temple
Visiting your grave I touched your tombstone
Still warm as I imagined   the way you were when you were here
Out of nowhere several winged shadows
flickered up my kimono sleeve

The Joys of Snow
When snow piles up
boys love to tumble into drifts
That's because mother's hand will appear
to help them out of the snow
into which they'd fallen
This morning too
impression after impression in the snow
where boys and their mothers
had tenderly embraced each other
under blue skies on the way to school

School from Afar*

I've come about a dozen years since finishing school
Looking back the school glitters tiny as a carved medallion
far beyond memory
In the carving classroom roofs merge their tiles
poplars twist and tremble in the wind
the teacher discusses something
as young faces listen absorbed
Someone near one window looks off
staring vacantly in my direction just as I did then
Ah I see him so clearly from here
Can he see where I am?

Starry Night

Jirô finished making his airplane
late at night
The entire family had gone to bed
only Mother stayed up at his side

Before going to bed
Jirô wanted to fly it just once
His mother had something to say about that
but he opened the front door and went out

The night cold
the street hushed
Jirô wound the propeller tight
held the plane steady with outstretched hands
and gently launched it

The plane flew off

higher and higher into the night sky
---- then he saw it glance off the second-floor eaves
and suddenly return on a crash course

The flight lasted only about a dozen seconds
but Jirô had seen many things
Stars shining throughout skies
he thought were black
Snow-white frost
on every neighborhood roof

Jirô continued to shiver inside
He felt he had seen the dreams of people throughout Japan
now sleeping soundly under stars under frost

Depressing Scene
Riding a train or the interurban
suddenly I find myself passing through an odd quarter of the city
a vast compound-like area
with one deteriorating factory wall after another
    discarded piles of iron
huge brick chimneys standing abreast and silently spewing smoke
a gas tank abruptly closing in on me
As though sketched onto an empty sky
    a radio tower appears faintly then disappears
I no sooner imagine that waves of roof tiles
    gradually recede below my window
than I find the tracks crossing above another viaduct

At such times I always sense
that without a single human being in the area
riders will naturally turn glum and feel drawn less to people
than to these gigantic depressing arrays of inorganic matter

Into Clouds on the Hill
I pet my dog
neck to back
back to tail

Ears lie flat
Coat glistening
belly bent in a bow

Ah my petting hand   wind in motion
the dog's stance bending into my strokes
the dog dashing through its stance

I unleash him into clouds on the hill
The dog bounds off full speed
like a flung stone you can't call back

The Dark
When the boy lights his lamp
squirrels scamper up the tree

He shines his lamp on the tree
The squirrels hurriedly hide in the tree top

When the boy points his lamp at the tree top
the squirrels flee into the sky
turn into stars

Into the Future
The father said:
Look! at this picture

at the sleigh dashing swiftly on
at the wolf pack in pursuit
see the reinsman frantically whipping the reindeer
see the traveler taking steady aim with a rifle
from behind the luggage
now a scarlet flash from the muzzle

The son said:
One wolf's downed   right?
Oh another sprang at the sleigh
but tumbled over backward covered with blood
It's night the endless steppes buried in snow
Can the traveler hold out?
How far has the sleigh to go?

The father said:
The sleigh flies like this till dawn
slaying yesterday's regrets one by one
dashing like Time into tomorrow
Soon beyond the path that sun will climb
streets of the future will glimmer into view
Look!
Sky on the hill already turning white

*The Japanese Skies**
Here on a cloudless morning in early May
standing on high ground
I look down toward the town in the distance
Its roofs and walls shrink gradually away from me
The roof tiles string together those nostalgic cameo–like shadings
seen in remembered picture books
Far and near   poles for the boys' festival are up

but no carp swim on them yet
only arrow pinwheels attached
Each arrow emits a golden patina
and as if by caprice
here and there a pinwheel creaks gently
but finally   was it a swirl of wind?
they all begin whirling furiously in unison
Ah how elegant those artless flashes!
Born and reared in Japan
I marvel all the more that the glare of her skies
still makes my eyes smart so

Old Poetry Collection
Using a soiled goose–quill pen
I once wrote some boyish verses
Gathered into a touching collection
the book was scattered by the world's winds
leaving me no copy

Years later . . .
I went searching for it
Yesterday in a dismal second–hand bookshop
I chanced upon that nostalgic self
Placed on a dusty shelf
he sold for fifteen *sen*

I thought I'd pay a *yen* for him
Holding the book and turning its pages
I saw sunset on the corner where once I lived
A faded dog came out barking
and leapt up on my shoulder

Mud–Colored Painting

I was painting a soldier
Steel helmet cocked to one side
pack and canteen and cartridge belt girding his chest
feet spread out as though responding to "Parade Rest!"
one extended hand gripping a bayoneted rifle
now he's grinning as if to greet someone

Then I added the setting
No shreds of cottony clouds no lonely rampart
no meditating crow none of the horizon's countless swells
Instead I smeared the background solid with a deep mud color
In the end I daubed out those two chilled marks
I'd hesitantly left unfinished under the rim of his helmet
------ those lashes now shadows over closed eyes

Horse at Dawn

Sounds of hooves gallop at me from beyond dreams
They stop before the house
My horse already come for me

I recall that I'm going out today
At once I leap from bed
I must get ready fast

Ah as I dress I hear him
impatiently kicking at the gate
vexatiously neighing shrill volleys

Then I see him
growing golden wings like the sun
in the frost-frozen dawn

Like Music*
In a few days I go to sea
I'll sail with young fellows on a four-masted barque
to southern isles with glowing sunken reefs
and beyond to the west through bands of trade winds
for harbors in the Philippines and along the China coast

Ah just think of how
joy will billow my sails the entire voyage!
That will set the tackle taut on my breast to singing
and make me run true under constellations of dream
rolling and pitching fiercely

Now I'm busily putting my feelings in order
I lash my flapping sails
take a careful fix like the ship's officer
inspect the compass   plot my course on the charts
stream the chip log   ring the ship's bell

Setting sail!   What spectacular days to come
Just now the season at the peak of its dazzling fete
In my tiny yard May flowers vie for color
and since morning summer butterflies as well
    have been fluttering effortlessly over the hedge
My heart too   like music   loud.

The Feet of Sailors
Sailors walk barefoot
over slick decks

Each morning the decks get
polished with sand and coconut

washed down with brine
swept by brooms
dried in the equatorial sun

No dirt in sea wind
That keeps sailors' feet
cleaner than if they'd walked on waves

Once
sailors standing on the foot ropes
worked high on a spar
and all eyes looked up at white soles
which seemed almost to mirror the seven seas

A Poet's Words*

The late Nakahara Chûya said
"You find no mermaids in the sea
In the sea
are only waves"

These words for some strange reason
remain vivid in my mind
If I chant them three times
mermaid faces peer out from between the sounds
If I mutter these words to myself
as I think back on a past cruise through southern seas
countless mermaid arms and tails appear and disappear
into sea's high blue swells

Or if I think dreamily of these words
when standing on a rocky shore under overcast skies
splashes of foam that dash against crags

sound like mermaids sighing

The late Nakahara Chûya's legacy to me:
The word *wave* has become mermaid
The word *mermaid*
has become wave

Dazzling Spring
Along the fence by the intersection
rows of cherry trees spread their branches
their leaves already bathed in gloomy shadows
During the day wind stirred   shadows paled then flickered
and a thorny caterpillar fell to the road
Shoes and wheels trampled it interminably
charging the area with a savage stench

Passersby knit their brows thinking
Ah the same thing may happen this year
Cheeks quivering girls dash through at full speed
tittering shrilly and clinging to each other
Old men and boys walk through deliberately feigning indifference
but soon pull up
and squeamishly brush off their sleeves and caps

I too pass through that place
deliberately ducking under the eaves on the other side of the street
half shutting my eyes as I walk by
To imagine that caterpillar not yet become a butterfly
somehow saddens even this dazzling spring day
Just then a stormy blast stirs overhead
raining on my shoulders things that gleam

Blossoms in Southern Seas

The moment we enter the trade wind belt
air abruptly turns refreshingly cool
Each day gentle southeasterlies blow
and the sea seems on the verge of dyeing my hands
the way it has melted the ink of its ultramarine
All twenty-six sails swelling
like gigantic white blossoms
our ship has bloomed on the southern seas
Caught in the reflections on those dazzling petals
we laugh together
squint through the sextant and
turning the helm
shake together with laughter
at every slack swell.

A Destitute Friend

He sat under the branches of a pear tree
As he talked he scooped water from the ewer
with his palm and let it drip away
he scooped it up and let it drip away
The drops made rings on the surface of the water
made ring on ring on ring
silently   soft as a harp

These sounds conveyed
as gracefully as possible
the sense of his pointed words

Waves

No sooner do I think that those swelling

seething waves might touch my palm
stretched out from the bulwark
than they curl and slip away from me
huge laconic waves
sending off neither foam nor spray

Beyond our heaving sailcloth and rigging
waves stand on tiptoe to steal glances of us
over the ventilators' shoulders over the heeling helm
Sometimes the waves suddenly raise their heads nearby
then slowly pass looking down at the deck
huge waves the shape of deep blue hills

One day quite unexpectedly
a chunk of one dolphin–shaped wave
leapt up on deck
Immediately I tried to stop it with my foot
but for some reason my head began to swim
Ah that dream–like instant

He vanished
Sun promptly dried the puddle
he had left behind

*Helm**

The huge helm at the stern seems
as weighty as something sprouted from waves
Two sturdy young sailors
heaving together
with all their might
turn it round and round•

I happen to look up at the mizzenmast
The ship turns
No the ship doesn't turn
Pivoting on the royal sail
clouds silently begin to turn
Little by little the sky the sea
yes the world begins to turn

Apples
Already time for dessert
The watch officer comes down from the spar deck
Before taking his place at table
he never fails to report
 Our course southwest by west
 Winds shifting now
 We're doing around six knots
The captain takes note and responds
 Well done
Sunset clouds pitching in the portholes behind them
all at table
silently pick up their knives

Plates go *clinkety clinkety*
Fourteen apples halved
For an instant air thickens with a heavily sweet–sour scent
Air thickens with the chokingly heavy sweet–sour scent
of grass
of trees
of land

Themes
Snow has stolen the sun

from children
Snow has stolen places to play
from children
Snow has stolen
colors and shapes of mountains and rocks trees and grass
from children
Snow has stolen bird songs
from children

Just how do you suppose children exist
through each positively ashen and monotonous half a year
with no sunlight no sound no color?

I have them write themes in class
Incessantly licking their stubby pencils
every last child conscientiously records only that
I woke up in the morning
I went to bed at night
I ate my meals

I feel as though powdery snow on mountains wrapped in wind
had swirled up from these pathetic blank pages
and fiercely flogged my forehead

Living Alone*
Walking half the day over snowy mountain trails
I reach home at twilight
even my mind chilled by shadows of snow

Wearily I cross my legs by the *irori*
get the wood smoking   warm my hands and feet
hang a kettle on the spit   heat some water•

In those moments before my tea is ready
I bend over to light a cigarette
Suddenly I feel the urge to turn and talk to someone
but say nothing when I realize I'm alone

I suppose it dropped from my clothing
that lump of snow
melting now by the hearth

High Village*
I live in a village high on a mountain top
so sun rises each morning
from low snow–decked hills
beyond the plain spread below
and shines from under my dream–greedy bed
Riding updrafts from the deep dell
birds struggle one by one like gasps
toward the eaves of my cottage
I always look down at their backs
but have yet to look up at their breasts

Since living in this high village
day after day I've been watching
my future pale

Tranquil Festival*
On a day when snow falls
that hamlet on the valley floor
holds a tranquil festival•

One hears
no drums
sees no festive lanterns
in homes
are only the sounds of mortars

Sons brandish huge pestles
Daughters twist off pieces of *mochi*
and offer them
to the mountain spirit's little shrine

Shouldering steep cliffs
the spirit dwells
in heaped–up snow
He dwells
silently breathless
in twilight's pale blue

White Pictures
I'd asked the children to paint pictures
titled "Spring"
The children mixed their own colors
but with nothing colored to paint sat bewildered

Just mountain after white mountain and
just undulating white fields and
only branch tips in sparse groves
piercing the snow here and there
through faint india ink shadows•

I colored one child's sky
a light cobalt
And then by mistake
plop   a yellow blur
between the still–damp branches

I instantly apologized for my mistake
but the children rather took pleasure in it
"Hey a witch hazel's bloomed!" they said
The children were delighted

North Country
Whenever a roof–bleached train
windows misted
slid like a fantastic chain of gloom
into the early winter station
I thought
----- Oh that much snow has fallen already
      in the north country

Now that I live in the north country
once it's winter   whenever
during the idle moments of a life
      shut in by icicles and swirling snow
I hear a distant steam whistle
I think
----- The snow those trains hauled in then
      was from this north country

I recall as well
the sun–starved eyes
of travelers who detrained on city platforms

And then I wonder
whether I now have such eyes

A Lovely Notion*
Nothing is more strikingly lovely
than the notion
that stars shine even in daytime skies
the way they sparkle in skies at night

Living on a mountain from time to time
I'm somehow entranced by that thought
And going deep into the hills
I peer intently through the surface of the pond

Then actually
I begin to see
the glimmer of countless stars starting to sparkle
from deep in the pond where sun had silently set

The Blue Chalkboard
Even if we can't buy pencils
we can write with our fingers so it's okay
Even if we don't have notebooks
we can write in the sky so it's okay

Both math tables and words in our readers
both sketches and essays
we write everything in the air with our fingers

Till the day we can buy
pencils and notebooks and things

let's calmly face the sky's chalkboard
and do our studies with fingers of chalk

The sky's chalkboard is huge and fun to write on
Even with every child in Japan writing
we could never fill it up

Day in and day out clouds whitely
wipe it clean for us

Magical Country*
Late each year
bunches of grapes cover entire expanses of rock
Here and there deep in the range
akebi fruit hang heavy
hidden in thickets on steep ravines
and in remote beech woods dusky even in daylight
matchstick mushroom coronas flare with rainbows
Also *shimeji maitake yamadori* and other countless mushrooms
blanket the roots of trees

Nature's cornucopia of crops
lies far beyond innumerable sheer cliffs and rocky screens
in a magical country no outsider has laid eyes on
a place known only to
the heads of mountain families

When autumn comes
house heads secretly visit their family hunting grounds
They stride through clouds   slip through mist
fill their shoulder baskets

and in the dead of night return home under stars

House heads certainly do not tell their secrets to others
But when the patriarch nears life's end
finally he reveals this secret to his son
His son in turn passes it on to the grandson
so generation after generation so long as they live in these hills
only the house head knows

Living in Remote Mountains
Trees grow on the inclines of untraveled gorges
Spring makes them bloom with artless flowers
and in fall they ripen tiny rounded fruit
Through those moments before winter
their leaves redden as furiously as fire
then presently they're buried under snow
The all-out performances
and the painfully mute spirits
of those nameless far-off mountain trees
pervasively occupy my mind these days

How abruptly the sun sets
on a mountain trail!
As I walk skies suddenly darken
Shadows that snuggle together from pleats in the incline
envelope me   dissolve the hamlet
shudder my spine with chills
Ah the lonely twilight . . .
imagining that I can still see
my eyes blur dreamily
like a bird's

Mother's Umbrella*
Mother
it's twenty days
since you passed on
Autumn rains fall drearily
in this mountain hamlet

To make a living
I go out through that rain
under this tiny umbrella
you left as a memento

After you aged
you never left the house
without your black–silk granny umbrella
brought all the way to this lonely northern mountain country
holding it up on your journey to the next world

This short–handled western umbrella
you kept in its hand–made cover
reminds me of a girl's parasol

Holding it up
no rain falls on my head or shoulders
and I feel I'm still with you

Besides since days long past
when I was still a child and you were young
until you became a grandmother passing your days serenely
you constantly cast tender love into our feelings

Now as though enveloped in the shadows of that love
my heart warms pitifully
and flows with indulgent memories

Mother
from under this tiny umbrella   I gaze now
at these icy passing showers that pelt the real world
at fall foliage on faraway rain–blurred hills

Tsurubé
In the foothills of a much higher mountain
one ridge beyond our hillside hamlet
lies a village with the lovely name
Tsurubé
On starry nights they say you can see Yamagata's lights
blinking in the basin twenty–five miles off
They say Tendô's lights are visible too
Tsurubé has just over thirty households
Blizzards blow more fiercely there than here
snow heaps up more deeply there than here
They've built a little branch school
where nine children's desks huddle numbly
in the middle of the snow–dusted floor
and a huge harmonium decorated with medieval carvings
squats ponderously near a window
If a visitor whimsically presses a key
the organ hums gently like a dream
It hums in tremolo
like the song of one who had long put up with solitude

*Hunting Matchstick Mushrooms**

Clawing over crags
cutting across ravines
how many miles have I hiked by now?

I found them again this year
in the glooms of a deep mountain woods
that drip at times with mist
More than an armful on a beech stump
lush with matchstick mushrooms
clumped tightly together   not a gap!

Just then
actually I'm not sure of the time
I saw the unspoiled vitality of countless haloes
whose sparklings reveal multicolored rainbows
in faint sunlight sifting through tree tops

What a mystical sight!
Despite having grown up in these mountains
I fold my arms and simply gape
Momentarily disinterested
I involuntarily sit on a fallen tree trunk
and   well   thinking I'd have a smoke
reach for the cigarette case in my sash

*Devastation**

Flames had enveloped the entire city
As the explosions became more distant
the safety of his huge collection of beloved books on English literature

gnawed intensely on Professor "D"'s mind
Driven off by flames   collar and cuffs singed
he had lost his home that night
so he rushed to the college through smoldering fires

Burned–down campus structures here and there
smoke still belching from rows of green trees
But when he stepped through the ruins and set foot in the shelter
his heart leapt at the glorious sight!
His ten–thousand volume library lined up on the shelves
as well–ordered as it had been the day before . . . .
Ecstatic   the professor unconsciously reached
to touch a title

At that moment every last book crumbled silently
to ash

Butterflies or Birds
Simply braiding leaves into their hair
casts green shadows over the children's brows
Then freckle–like spots of verdure
appear on hands on feet all over their bodies

When these children enter a mountain thicket
they at once become invisible
as though hidden by the hues of branches and leaves
Then suddenly they stand up
from grass clumps along the path
from behind trees•

It startles me dreadfully
almost as though
butterflies had fluttered up before me in the woods
or I'd discovered nearby a little bird

Class Log
Morning   before class begins
a girl raises her hand
---- *Teacher the swallows are gone*

I climb up by the window
check the nest under the eaves and then
taking out my class log
add this postscript to yesterday's entry
    September 28: Swallows depart
    The mountain chilly now

Flowercore
Every girl was smiling
Not a one said
I like you or I hate you
they simply left me one by one
smiling in silence

These multi–petaled smiles
ever on my palm!
I pluck them now
one by one each to the flowercore
Having lost their smiles
only scent survives

The Lonely Universe *
Only starry skies dimly lit
the ground so inky I can't tell where it is
I hear many singing frogs
seething up from the dark gloom
I hear them yes I hear them
their furious clamor
unchanged since remote antiquity

Earth spins stealthily toward dawn
night after night leaving those clamors in the wake of its orbit
one bundle of songs after another
as though they were serial nebulae

Somewhere in the lonely universe
frogs sing again today
hordes   and hordes
of singing frogs.

The Lunar Calendar
As night
follows day
the lunar calendar visits the Japanese countryside
when the solar calendar leaves

"Second New Year" on the lunar calendar
visits this hilltop village too
amid February's desolately heaped–up snows

Houses having tightly secured their doors
crouch behind snowsheds

but children bring sprigs of dogwood from the hills
skewer dumplings on them   suspend folded cranes
to decorate beams above the smoldering open hearth
Sprigs slender   red dumplings round and white
plain paper cranes mirroring flames
How dreamily wistful!

Two young men
stand facing a peach or is it a persimmon tree
One raising an axe addresses the tree
----- *Will you bear? Or won't you?*
   If not down you come!
then drives his axe into the trunk
In pain the flustered tree top screams
----- *I'll bear for you*
   I'll bear for you

Indeed when fall comes
the tree bends deep with fruit.

POETRY PUBLISHED BETWEEN

1948 and 1974

Working Girl*
After the drone of the belt stops
in that workshop at the foot of the slope
the girl will pass my place again
on her way home

not weary from not upset with
her daily labors
her lively footsteps
regular as clock ticks

Whenever she approaches
even the mind at my desk
bursts suddenly with energy
as though its spring had been re–wound

Her footsteps pass
Mixed with them
the muffled clatter
of an aluminum lunch pail

Telephone Pole
Whenever I put my ear to the telephone pole
it was ringing
It was ringing loudly *konng*

Whenever I stood away from the pole
I no longer heard that sound
Skies blue I felt lonely

Whenever I put my ear again to it
naturally the pole was ringing

It was ringing loudly *konng*

When I looked up at the sky ear to the pole
the sky was ringing too
It was ringing a clear *konng*

Snowy Field*
A child stands on the slope
holding a bamboo *wappa*

He stares intently
The fields thoroughly desolate
everywhere only snow
But   the child knows
what whiteness hides

Soon in the distance
two meager dots begin taking shape
Above each dot two slender things that move . . .
then around them a faint circle
seemingly sketched by shadows
breaks the surface of the snow

Taking aim
the child hurls his *wappa*
It *wooshes* through the air
quite like a swooping hawk

Startled the hare leaps up
It tumbles down the slope trying to escape
becomes the child's catch

On a Mountain Path
Paralleling the mountain's pleats
a deep gorge snakes along silently bend on bend
twilight mists seething over one of its flanks

Something rustles behind me
now and then as I pass through
At each sound I look back
I wonder if a bird is there but there is no bird
I wonder if it's an animal but no animal either
Then at last I realize it's the sound of dirt
sloughing off the incline

I notice gritty dirt
slithering incessantly down the precipice
bits at a time just tiny bits
Were they dislodged by breezes that barely stir?
by shudders from my footfalls?
or for no reason at all?

Rows of cedars darken my destination
Suddenly as though he materialized out of nowhere
I notice a child strolling in front of me
As he idles along shouldering an empty bamboo basket
infinite solitude closes in on him
How very tiny he seems!

Evening Mist
It wanders out of evening mists on the hill
It tags along unnoticed by people on the path
It flies around a while then settles on a grass blade
or flits up to a tree again and rests under a leaf

Each time it glares over its shoulder and waits for someone
then shadows endlessly him

Once I too saw one
gleaming in speckles of gold and green
an eerie phantom–like winged bug
smaller than a cricket

At nightfall
a villager trudging that long and desolate way
struggled to the gate of his house   abruptly paled
and died without a word
No one knows why
but people say that only someone about to die
can see the demon fly leave him
and flee free into the dark of night . . . .

Fox Fire
A single glittering light
on the steep mountainside beyond the gorge . . . .
The light busily reproduces itself
seems to form a horizontal row   vanishes abruptly
then turns into a vertical line
That too vanishes in a twinkling
and darkness returns

This phenomenon they call
"fox fire"
People talk about how the fox dashes through the heart of the hills
bone splinters in his mouth
They say too that whenever the fire appears
the fox is right behind you•

Even if true   I wonder why it happens
Oh those rustic cruciform blinks
that some hunted mountain beast kindles --
sorcery pregnant with pathos!

Carossa and Rilke
In his *Romanian Diary*
Carossa wrote as follows
about a young girl suffering from consumption
in the aftermath of war's destruction
  "The scant oxygen in her entire body seemed
   concentrated in those hugely opened eyes"
If at that moment
he had inadvertently approached her with the flame of love
her eyes would have burnt away in an instant
and she would have gone to heaven

They say Rilke's eyes were always limpidly blue
profoundly absorbing imagery
without harboring even a hint of a shadow
What if we had sailed a boat on a lake of that hue?
Dread would quickly have driven us insane

Like a Lamp
She who loved me all her life
she who continues loving me
my mother   my wife

Mother's love brightened me half a century
then flickered out three years ago
Shadows gathered in a corner of my heart

I shed my tears in them

My wife has loved me for twenty years
and untiringly loves me still

Possibly she will outlive me
and shine alone
like a lamp
in a room without a mate

Unspoken Love
Near the towering summit
when I pass by over dense heaped–up snow
or under bowed trees bathing in the sun
I suddenly begin reminiscing
about Mother no longer with us
about my wife at home

or about those modest acts of kindness
by women who came my way
and passed quickly by without a trace

Memories of unspoken love
mellowing in Nature
hum at times through my mind like the wind . . .

Greenfinch
Did my brief remarks
discourage you so much my young friend?
In the letter I received this morning
your cramped characters tediously recorded bewilderment
thoughts going this way going that way

self–confidence in disarray
your mind still immature
this whole affair pathetic
as pitiful as a bird downed in flight
and dragging itself along the ground

At this moment a greenfinch
flies above the head filled with these thoughts
Alighting atop an oak tree
it immediately begins to shrill
But unlucky for the finch I have my air gun with me
Actually I'd come here to shoot a bird

The butt settles quickly against my shoulder
I place my finger on the trigger
Oh!   reminded then of this morning's letter I shoot the finch
whose silhouette casts a shadow over my thoughts

Unfamiliar Locale
I've come hundreds of kilometers
just sitting still
just wrapped in ruminations reaching into yesterday
or just sound asleep untroubled as paper
Though I did not move by willing movement
the train had carted me off in an instant

Whatever does distance mean?
I'm in an unfamiliar locale right now
but more often than not actually forget I am

If I lean over the rail of a bridge spanning a finger of the lake
and look down into a school of transparent fish

    meandering through the water
or stare into the clouds the smoke the hills mirrored there
I'm instantly and wearily aware of what distance means

By a Pond
Numerous whitebait swimming
in clear water under the bridge
swimming aimlessly
each aglitter with life
breaking the water like flashes of light
Unfortunately they're as transparent as glass chips
so they leave no shadows on the sandy bottom
That's quite like the trivial rambling thoughts
incessantly coming and going through my mind
Although piteous   bitter   painful
and filled with the quandaries of life
they too leave no trace in memory

Flame
Down the afterdeck's spiral staircase
where the mizzenmast reaches straight up
a small quivering oil lamp
with a bean–shaped flame
each night the only light after taps

Before daybreak at 4:15
the young lampman off watch in steerage
descends the hatch over which stars flicker faintly
and never fails to blow out the flame

One morning

when as usual I was passing by
the lampman came along pale
shivering
a fish just pulled from the brine
spray and rain dripping everywhere from him
his bare feet leaving puddle–prints . . .

The instant he neared the lamp
its flame spontaneously died

Night Journey
Somebody
between the rails and the coach
The grating and grinding of bones
indicate that someone's flesh is being crushed
where steel bites into steel
Ah wherever that huge hulk whirls and hurtles on
we find unending human shrieks
Weary–faced riders have shut their eyes
but do they really fail to hear those cries?
Eyes closed I too pretend I do not hear

Crow Flock
Because I often pick the last car
when I ride a train
and take a seat facing the rear
I can enjoy watching
rails that dash pell–mell way from me
the present squeezed moment by moment into the past
and at length folded into loss

I sometimes stand up front

on a rushing interurban
Then I see vague far-off forms start taking shape
The future incessantly moving into the present
and new futures unraveling from the cores of unfamiliar skeins
That experience enthralls me too

Yes but why should it?
From time to time
crows flock on crossties   atop signal towers
Although the crows tend not to surrender their space
they fly up ponderously in the nick of time
then settle down again

Visible ahead
visible to the rear
they stand motionlessly deep in thought among the rails
no   among the dreary hours of life

News from the Cape*
Over the last two or three days here
the sea has been intensely transparent
the sky pure blue

Turning up my heels
each day I dive
deep into the sea and
marvelous!   marvelous!
before I know it I'm in the sky
Through my diving goggles
I can see the sun between a cleft in the rocks•

Holding my spear high
I rush toward the light
Then somewhere
a harp starts singing serenely
and a file of fish circles the sky
as in an ancient Egyptian mural

Reaching out gingerly
I pry off sea mussels and abalone
from behind the sun

Night Trees*
Before falling asleep at night
it's somehow delightful to think of trees
those enigmatic tree shapes
breathing high into the starry dark of open skies . . . .

I think of as many trees seen during the day as I can
That *hinoki* I noted somewhere along a fence
coiling up exactly like van Gogh's cypresses
that huge aspera in the park somewhat like a Chagall canvas
every one charged with sunlight with rustlings
and layering the lively chatter of birds into the arabesques
that leaves and branches make . . . .

And then suddenly I become aware that at this very moment
the trees utterly lose their songs their glare
and mysteriously turn into silent ebony shadows
marshaled in my imagination . . .

My consciousness

melts gradually into sleep
I lose my me
and in that loss
another self arises

I hold my green lantern ready
Opening the shutters without a sound
Just like that I soar off into the night skies
my long *yukata* fluttering in the air

I'm already in the midnight sky
Without a wing flap I move from one tree clump to another
treading gently on the tree tops
Illuminating gaps in branches so mystic and curious to me
I swim off under the glitter of stars . . . .

Stars[*]

In his prose poem "Stars"
the poet Alphonse Daudet
borrows a shepherd's expression
to convey the nighttime hush of the Alps
He says that in the skies each star breathes
that he can even hear vegetation growing

Incidentally the northern mountain village
    where I lived until just two or three years ago
was precisely a locale like that
The instant night fell earth turned absolutely black
Deep in the heart of the darkness mountain flumes roared
From the opposite direction
stars emitted light as fierce as flames

My place

sat on a bluff high on a hillside overlooking the plain
so the glitter of stars was never simply overhead
I could scrutinize stars below eye level
on three sectors of the horizon
When I thrust out a hand
my palm took up the same space as the stars
If I stretched out a leg
it seemed that the sole of my foot could stomp the stars
My existence was simply a matter
of getting up or sleeping amid millions of stars

When winter snows melt
mountainsides suddenly color with spurts of green
Night reeks powerfully then
with grass and trees and stars
with vegetation with minerals . . . .

Mars -- Venus -- Sirius -- the Polestar
the Big Dipper -- Scorpio -- Cygnus
whichever one I observed
I felt that nothing inched more into intimacy than the stars
and at the same time nothing felt as increasingly remote
Midnight   closing eyes heavy with watching
I drift pleasantly into sleep
In my mountain dwelling
I sleep perfectly sound   dreamless
till bird twitters in the forest
merrily announce the dawn . . . .

With but a Few Words
It should be possible to snare a poem
with but a few words
only a few simple words

no more than children have in hand
just by inventively weaving them together

It would be a poem I'd not regret
one probing deeply into daily life
to track down streams of feeling and the flow of thoughts
swimming life's transparent depths
those shadows of man's unique mind
shadows that one ultimately scoops up like little fish

images freshly bursting with life
flipping in the net
sometimes ready to slip through the mesh of words

Personally moved to tears
by the risks
how beyond my dreams
if only I could convey this experience naturally to someone else!
I'm always thinking   that's the poem I'd love to write

Midnight Mirror
Midnight mirror
that hushed glass
mirroring but one corner of the room
A glass that nobody looks into and yet
someone's eyes   no no the eyes of the whole world
focus on and stare frantically into it

At that moment a young girl abruptly appears
and slips off her clothes before the mirror

------ wondrous shivers tingling her spine
actually entranced in the pallid light
gazing intently at her naked reflection

Taking a step forward
the cold glass before her
she kisses her other self
One second Two seconds Three seconds
The girl stands motionless
------ then abruptly steps back   turns
snatches her pajamas from the wall   vanishes

After that not a stir
Hushed again
the glass mirrors the curtains
An empty room and yet the eyes of the whole world
merge with and stare without a blink into that glass
The mirror stands at the focus of those eyes
its lipstick smudge alone
lingering flower–like till dawn

The Sea of Okhotsk
A friend told me
"I'd really like to show you the Sea of Okhotsk"
He said "Until you've seen it
you're not qualified to write about the North!"
He even noted "The very colors of the sea deserve amazement
They're deep with melancholy and swell massively . . .
no no they're totally beyond description"
I asked him "Would you say they're like the back of a fur seal?"
Closing his eyes he said "Right but not exactly"•

A letter came from my friend
so I went to Hokkaidô and took the trip with him
We went from Sapporo to Asahikawa
    from Asahikawa we stopped at Kitami
from Kitami we headed for Kushiro
Finally Abashiri ------ I saw waves from the coach window
The Sea of Okhotsk

Yes the Sea of Okhotsk
but quite an ordinary body of water
the offing bright   cattle roaming the strand
"Is this Okhotsk?" I asked
"Yep" he acknowledged "This is it"
He said no more
When the train stopped he rose from his seat
"Shall we go pick sweetbriars or something?"

The Man Who Encountered a Bear *
Rumbling down the slope
something blackly black came sliding along
poised on its haunches   front paws raised . . . .
A bear! The moment I realized it
he tumbled sideways into the cover of some bamboo bushes
------ I'd no sooner thought he was gone than I saw him again
scurrying away from me up the mountain trail

I had set out walking again
Resolved not to look back
I moved deliberately
but told myself I didn't need to walk so calculatedly slow
I took a cigarette from my pocket
finally found a match and lit up

Half a kilometer down the mountain I met a wood cutter
He badgered me about my pale face
"A bear!" I told him
"Frightening?"   After consideration I replied
"It was certainly uncanny"

Indeed no deception there
Quite an eerie sensation
When the beast looked at me with those eyes
innocent yet burning brightly deep within
I immediately sensed reality fade
No no not exactly   I sensed rather that
Time from an entirely other dimension
had crossed the Time where I'd existed
    in which I continue to exist
an unknown Time breathing and pulsing wildly like the wind
Unexpectedly absolutely unexpectedly
I stood at their intersection

Instantly the mountain stream stood still
In response to the hush the forest the grass the earth the rocks
briefly echoed a shriek
resounding even now within my head

A Crane
A crane soars
over the blue sea

like a sooted and shabby umbrella
singing sadly

That bubble reputation

so long enjoyed
turns to shadow   slips away
mirrored black
on creases in the brine.

The Tree in Me
I don't know when it began but a tree has taken root in me
It grows through my growth
Spreading branches from my growing limbs
its leaves thicken into shapes of grief

I no longer go out
I no longer speak to anyone
not to Mother not even to friends . . . .
I'm becoming the tree in me
No no I've already become that tree

I stand quietly far beyond the fields
Whenever I greet morning sun
whenever I look off after clouds fired by sunset
my silence glitters
my solitary self sings

Horizon
Not even a galleon at anchor
and yet an antique boat came rowing toward me
Dangling pigtails cutlasses at their sides
the men on board disappeared over dune–like silhouettes

Once again . . .
a single mermaid spewed

from the endless petitions
of sea's many hundreds of complaints
of waves' many thousands of sighs
She no sooner leapt onto the beach and glanced up at empty skies
than at once she rode off on a receding wave

Ah that horizon folding up the distant future
But only cheerless phantoms of the past
dash at me now from there

The Hostage Sea -- On Ocean Day*
Fettered by a line of steel chains
she's been dragged toward the offing
year after year   meter by meter
Eyes moist with the hue of seaweed
stare intently at the horizon off Japan

A sea that breathed in our youth
that was once so very full of life!
But violated now
and heartlessly polluted
her breasts her entire body paralyzed by poisons!

This morning Ocean Day visits the port again
Beyond scattered banners and the soaring of gulls
we see the bright wake of a waterway
never to return

Sea Beast
The ocean glitters under sunset
Oh that gigantic fish who eyed me for an instant

leaping high with a *whoosh* through flying foam!

A year since then and thousands of knots
I'm sure that fellow even now
swims somewhere in a globe–girdling current
now or then recalling me . . .
just as his face comes to my mind from time to time
as I swim the congested waves of life on land

You wonder why?   Actually in a dream last night
he unexpectedly stopped by to greet me
With a somewhat grizzled and weary expression
he wiggled his fins without a word
then promptly plunged into that endlessly expanding sea
deep in the depths of my consciousness

*That Fellow Within**
The old days were wonderful
I craved only the things
that I craved

Life is different now
That fellow within me
who wears a face like mine but is not me
craves everything

That fellow has divested the sea of women
wrestled saké from the skies
stripped verdant potentials
from future time

Oh I've taken every part of him

pressed the parts together and discarded them
Chomping and gulping
I bolted them down

Good riddance!
That fellow in me is not me
A monster
I can't let him go on living here

The Coral Sea
Huge waves surge against the prow
making endless furrows
Gleams that differ from yesterday's
shadows that differ from those the day before that
prance over every
emerald pulse

From those gleams
from those shadows
things that dance up nimbly   quickly
things that stream by now and again in the wind
grazing funnels and portholes
Are they sea gulls?
Flying fish?
No no they're leaves
cheerless withered leaves
scattering over the autumn sea

Vision
Anchor up from the seabed
spitting brine
No it's no anchor

That's a woman
dangling from the end of the chain
an absolutely naked woman
smeared with mud   trussed up in seaweed
Look! How pathetic
Isn't she frozen blue and utterly spent?
And yet she's winched up
relentlessly
dried in sea breezes   arms and legs folded
fixed with a clang inside the anchor ring
No no inside the men's minds
Already a frozen vision
she's taken like that to sea

Autumn Dreams
Evening insects hum
Whenever I hear their voices
my body exists outside the window
where I'm lying on the grass

Evening rain falls
Whenever I savor its scent
my mind exists beyond the door
where I'm lying on the ground

Both insect voices and the scent of rain
saturate my spine steep my head and then
finally falling asleep
I have forlorn dreams the whole night

In my dreams my house becomes decrepit
rots and collapses before my eyes

(My wife?)
(The children?)

Dawn
My cries wake me
Rain stops
Winds blow

Poetry
I wake in the middle of the night
Detesting the glow of electric lamps
I light a candle

I prefer a candle
because I hope to kindle myself in it
because I want to refashion myself
beyond its flickering point

I haven't stirred yet
but I can clearly see
the flame nibbling into night
The more it nibbles night away
the more I see my agonies lighting up
I can also see fine dirt and dust break through the halo
then be consumed by the flame
The more dirt and dust the flame devours
the more I find this night hour purged

At last . . .
a moment of ecstatic calm
I stand up and pass through the flame
The candle dies away
but I become a butterfly at dawn

changed into a chilled   into an absolutely solitary butterfly
at the dawning of a winter day . . . .

***Minato Ward, Nagoya**   *(Memo on the Isé Bay Typhoon)*
Mackerel bob up from the kitchen
enter the alleyway through a window and   revived
swim down the street between slanting utility poles
heading vigorously for the estuary for the sea
Deep under riled–up eddying waters
    women
    children
    old people
who had instantly exchanged their souls with the fish
surface here and there and   towed off on rafts
pass again today
under twilight eaves holding their breath
Tomorrow cremation under sunny skies

Illusion in the Reef
The chalky coral grove
comes floating transparently to the surface
like a sunken image
deep within a poem
A single baby shark undulates
through coral tips sunlight streaming everywhere
No that's a boot
an airman's boot already beginning to dissolve
like a shadow like kelp

In the Corridor of Omaezaki Lighthouse*
Soon I guess
the light will begin its revolutions here
They say that every twenty seconds
Omaezaki's million–plus candle power lamp
sweeps some forty knots of offing

Near the beam's reach
griefs bearing the silhouette of a younger me
unexpectedly drift my way
from waves far on the horizon where light stubbornly lingers
I was certain they would be there   yes
they should have been there
bearing the silhouette of a younger me

Face with Ants*
Ants crawl over eyelids
Then that nearby hollow suddenly gathers shadows
as though engraved

Ants lick the inner corners of the eyes
From there they go straight down the cheek
------ and as I watch   that nearby hollow
deepens as though scooped out

Ants circle that mole by the mouth
Then they scurry into breathless nostrils
They won't show themselves again
They may never reappear

Oh the shame of staring so
Oh the shame of being so stared at

Tenth Floor Bar in the "Q" Hotel
A panorama beyond the glassed-in lobby
spectacle of lights and stars sparkling the spring night
Despite being confronted by that fantasy
my mind no longer stretches its wings

Had it been the me of a decade back
I suppose I would promptly have booted myself
    off this lofty structure
and started flapping in the air

Whenever had I changed and why?
In the soaring stance that is Poet
my future stands empty something reflected on closed eyes
now simply a space-time continuum indifferent to me

I am an old bird motionless on its perch
highball fizzing vacuously in my hand

A Mortified Figure*
Dusk's silhouette reaches from beyond the cosmos
It's neither earth's silhouette crossing the moon
nor moon's silhouette veiling the sun
One day that shadow will surely edge toward me as well
When it shrouds my eyes and ears and clogs my breath
I'll leave this self behind
chaperoned by a flea

That self with long fingernails the hue of rotted leaves
Who would lift its white face cover again
to peer at the mortified figure on display a figure no longer myself?

A feeble wild elephant hurries away from his herd

barges through the jungle   works his way upstream   passing
    through the waterfall
deep into an unexplored grotto to abandon himself

Far beyond the horizon black smoke rises
Soldiers crouching low   rifles at port   step over a man
face–down his outstretched arms joined fly–like at the palms
He does not praise his God Allah
He's a mute immovable carving engraved on burning sands
his mortified figure now
exposed to the eyes of the world

Such Scenes . . .
Railroad tracks generally
run near estuaries

There
the river widens its bed forming sandbars
Flow pinched and splitting into several forks
the river has already surrendered its shape

As the train crosses the trestle
my eyes involuntarily look downstream
Land breezes melt into sea breezes
fresh water mixes with tide water
skies overhead unite with skies over the sea
off toward where they redden expansively

Any flying creature here
will already be a sea bird
Whatever exists disappears
and transforms into something new
I love such scenes

The River
The old man lived his whole life on the river

Standing in the gorge's rapid rush
Squatting on the shoreline off a back street
Mooring his boat in that reed clump under the bridge

Always gazing at the surface of the water
his eyes fixed on his float
motionless against the flow
yet actually swept along by it

Both his thoughts and his life
swept downstream with clouds and wind and tree shadows
toward the river mouth toward the sea
destined for that timeless time beyond all things

One day the old man no longer appeared
At one spot where he had fished
a boy has dropped his line

Waterfowl
He remains motionless
in the pointless boisterousness of the screened enclosure
almost a part of the concrete crag
as he squats in that corner by the cool waterspout

A shabby inconspicuous smallish waterfowl
but what amazing vitality of flight he compresses in his pose!
At times   no periodically
he puffs his feathers up as though irritated
Once they return to normal
he leans forward ready for anything•

Then he stretches his wings
He spreads those phantom–like wings
farther and farther endlessly farther
Ah that instant dizzies me

But the bird does not fly
He folds up his wings closes his eyes
once again becoming motionless as though asleep

The Hunters and I*
I
We cut through thickets on the slope
away from paths that people use

In the inky dark
tree–shaded lush grass high enough to hide in
Look
bent grass tips
the snapped ends of little twigs

This is an *utsu*
a trail that only animals use
    (No no the secret path I take
    when I end up baffled about something)

This is not the only *utsu*
There's a network
linking hills and mountain streams
Near the heights where we'd climbed following one fellow
lay the lair of a beast polishing his tusks the cliff his canopy
ferns strewn over a bed covered with cedar greens

(Or is the beast myself?)

Oh! The far–off yelps of contending hounds
signal it's time
to release the safety catches on our rifles

II

I heard that for a number of years one survived
with my round
deep in his thigh
and that these hunters had brought him down
two hills away from here
That happened yesterday
    (I too -- plugged with a round of frustration . . . .)

It's no longer necessary to continue tracking
the one I shot today
I figured that around midnight
he'll surely come down to the mountain stream

Moon was up
Sure enough . . .
he emerged from a clump of weeds like a half–shadow
tottering as he approached the water's edge
I heard slurping sounds
so I supposed he was drinking

Then no sooner had he raised his head
letting out a flute–like sigh
than he tumbled in a heap to the ground

III
We used to haul the wild boar down from the mountain

slit its belly open there and roast its entrails on the fire
The whole party then partook of them

Oh yes before eating
we'd take a slice of his liver and stick it to a tree in the copse
    (I pierce my liver with a pen point)
and everyone offered prayer
Not a man among us had the slightest idea
which god we folded our hands to . . . .

    You died so nice for us today, *right!*
    Do it again tomorrow, *right!*

Only echoes from the mountain stream responded
Merging with them the wind ----- (my mind)
groaned past like moans
through vacant skies above the faraway ridge

The Stream -- Tale of an Old Hunter
A stag broke through the greenery
and pranced out on the opposite shore
obliquely upstream from me

About to step into the water
he turned gracefully around
then headed downstream
dashing over the riverbank at full speed

What speed!
Under his vaults the river instantly
reversed its flow•

On this shore hunters
their rifles lined up
simultaneously opened fire
but not a one hit the target

Finally when he came directly in front of me
I brought him down with my trusty single–shot rifle . . . .

As it soaked up the fallen stag's antlers
the river began again
flowing toward its mouth

*Dreams I See in the Sea**
Wanting money to buy a calf
I went to sea right out of middle school
worked my way up from apprentice deck hand in twelve years
and finally became an able–bodied seaman
Now I'm the quartermaster
Mornings and evenings I take the helm   check our bearing
and at times lapse into those precious dreams I had so long ago
The expansive sea turns into pasture
ruddy clouds become milch cows

*Abalone**
Plunging precipitously in the buff
at an acute angle direct for the seabed
with neither air tank nor flippers
there she is -- an intrepid Itoman–style harvester of abalone

Born in the Gotô Islands floating in the ocean west of Kyushu

"N–ko" dives deep into the rough Genkai Sea
to help her father reel in squid lines
After six years in a Hakata shop
she had returned to the Islands and once again became a diver

Early this spring she appeared
unexpectedly in my hospital room
more huge fresh abalone than hands could hold
crammed into her travel bag
one strap torn

At that moment I lay flat on my back scrutinizing
the Roentgen photograph the hospital head was explaining to me
The X–ray traced in my chest cavity
that very old darkly–sedimented sea of my youth
By now what was left of that longed–for barque
already scuttled
had been utterly transformed into rusted keel and ribs

> Look! It's cloudy there
> No doubt evidence of your old disease

Instantly blood that raised no cry
responded to his words

> No No   Surely that's the shadow of my attachment to the sea
>   now a barnacle
> bonded firmly to my ribs
> Doctor can't you see
> the swimming silhouette of N–ko   metal pry in hand
> an underwater butterfly threading sinuously
> and flashing through the grove of my ribs?

Golden Cub*

I need neither precious stones nor marble statues
I want only a lion cub glowing with glints of gold
romping over noon–time wave–washed African bluffs
Those cubs have vanished now from the plaintive dozing eyes
of that old fisherman in Hemingway's novel
Ah those innocent lion cubs -- a single one will do . . . .

My wife grew old without bearing a child
I feel no sense of loss
because I've been thinking
how nice if a lion would spring from her womb
a male lion king of the distant savannah
legs bursting with sinewy aggressiveness his mane inspiring awe
though latent with potential never ever
surrendering those spots on his soft coat
Rolling like a ball he'll begin to frisk at my feet
At times showing his little fangs and claws
he'll growl and nip at my neck or claw the back of my hand
------ in no time he'll be taking wapiti or buffalo
I want such a lion cub glowing with the luster of gold
a cub the image of what he was at birth

In my mind I'd like to nourish
his innocence his ferocity his warmth
so long as I have life

Snares*

There are men there are women
attracting each other being attracted
wandering near places lush with grass

exchanging love poems writing and enjoying poetry   stories . . . .
Once you've inadvertently walked into some thicket
you worsen the agonies the grudges the tears and in the end
you'll kill your partner and snuff out your own life

Listen to their cries of grief to their screams!
Doesn't every conceivable ploy
exist in snares set up by God
whom I've not yet had the pleasure of meeting?

Let's move ahead with our eyes opened
It's best to step lightheartedly over snares
Even if by chance your foot gets caught in one
it won't do to shout and thrash about fecklessly
I'd rather you imitate the courage and determination of the hyena
who escapes by chewing off his own paw
True love starts there

*Strolling the Dunes**

As I think of you
you are far off
your shadow small my voice unable to reach you
soaked up by the volume of the backdrop

You retreating
I pursuing
Second by second however
somehow the unobstructed space between us increases

What's the essence of the drab resignation
of those awesome silences
those gigantic irresistible heaps?•

Wind blows
Sands stir
Waves lap the shore

Only sea unfolds its songs into headings through the blue
I do not wish to take . . . .

White Magnolias on My Mind
Their flowers bloom more unspoiled each year
last year's purer than those of the year before
this year's purer than last year's
On a leisurely back street   a blaze of blossoms had kindled
the glowing tree top   which the owner of that shabby little yard
and tree itself had waited with so much hope
Perhaps similar blossoms also inconspicuously ignite
copses here or there on the slopes of unknown distant gorges
but those would be wild magnolias   or *kobushi*
At daybreak in early spring
in the skies—moon and stars covertly kiss
from the ground—the scent of flared buds rises high
At that moment   as white magnolias flowered
far more beautifully more sadly by the year
my life was draining gradually away . . .
soon to make such worldly things invisible to me.

SUPPLEMENTARY

Notes on the Poems

Entries appear in alphabetical order under the name of the poem. Information below derives from notes in the *Works,* from correspondence and interviews with the poet and his widow, as well as with others in both Toyohashi and Iwanezawa.

Abalone -- Itoman, a small town known for its excellent divers, lies on the west coast of Okinawa about ten miles due south of Naha. N-ko refers to Nishimura Masuko (Maruyama "disguises" names by taking the next letter of the alphabet, so that M̲asu–k̲o becomes N–ko). The Gotô Islands are situated off the coast of Kyushu directly to the west of Sasebo. The Genkai Sea is off the west coast of Saga, a province in the northwest corner of Kyushu. Hakata, a metropolis in northern Kyushu, currently serves as the terminus of the "bullet train" (*shinkansen*). "Metal pry" renders *fuguse,* a tool divers use to pry shellfish from rocks. Ms. Nishimura had initially approached Maruyama some years before the event described in this poem to ask for his comments on the free verse about the sea that she had written.

Devastation -- Professor "D" refers to Doi Kôchi (1886–1979), who at the time Maruyama wrote this poem (1947) chaired the English department at the national university in Sendai (Tôhoku Daigaku). Maruyama met Doi while lecturing in Sendai on modern Japanese poetry.

Dreams I See in the Sea -- A naval quartermaster (assistant navigator or helmsman) is in charge of navigation equipment.

Face With Ants -- The picture of an American soldier killed in Vietnam provided Maruyama with the inspiration for this poem. Notice that the poet, too, has a facial mole near his mouth.

God Who Wept -- The Japanese word *kami*, which I render in this instance as God with a capital "G," defies English translation. In daily usage, *kami* can refer either to dead spirits or to the living great -- including military heroes. The term *kami* registers a person's sense of awe, whether in response to a living or a dead person, to a spectacular boulder or tree, and the like. Fundamentally, *kami* describes a subjective reaction to the presence of greatness or to the numinous.

Golden Cub -- Maruyama refers here to Hemingway's parable, *The Old Man and the Sea* (1952). Fishing alone in the Gulf Stream, the old man had not caught anything for almost three months when he finally landed an eighteen–foot fish. After days of struggle and suffering he finally got the fish back to port, but by then sharks had devoured most of it. The last words of the novel describe how the old man, trying to sleep off his weariness, "was dreaming about lions." As a psychological image, note that lions -- aside from their fierceness and power -- represent latent passions and the perils of the unconscious mind.

Gun Emplacement -- The gun, a coastal defense mortar captured during the Russo–Japanese War (1905), had been set up to commemorate the attack on Port Arthur led by General Nogi Maresuke (1849–1912). The memorial stood on Kudan Hill, just off the Palace grounds. Maruyama said that its sad state of disrepair reminded him of his personal feelings at that time.

Helm -- Each mast on a full–rigged sailing vessel has a royal sail, the second highest sail under the skysail; sailors designate each royal by its mast: the Fore Royal, the Main Royal, and the Mizzen Royal.

High Village -- For another description of the setting for this work, see the 1951 poem "Stars," annotated below. Maruyama said in interviews that "High Village" resulted from his realization that the kindness of the people of the north enticed him to become ensconced forever in Iwanezawa. He feared that remaining there would end his career as a poet. In the last line of the poem, he uses the word "fate [*unmei*]"; with his permission I substituted "future," for that is what he had in mind. Unfortunately, "future" does not capture Maruyama's sense of incomplete control over his life. At the school where he taught, a marker suggests the metaphoric dimensions of this and other works describing Iwanezawa's altitude. The sign laconically states: "Elevation 400 meters."

Hostage Sea -- On Ocean Day -- Ocean Day was celebrated on July 20. Maruyama said that he had imagined the Pacific felt "lonely" because almost the entire Japanese fleet, including most of her merchant marine vessels, had been sent to the bottom during World War II.

Hunters and I -- An earlier version of this poem appeared as "*Hantaa no hanashi* [Tale of a hunter]" in *Shiki [The Four Seasons]* (August 1968). It was then prefaced by what is now the independent poem "*Nagare* [The Stream]," about a man hunting deer. The wild boar *[shishi]* stands as a universal symbol of courage, tenacity, and fierce perversity. Boars are very hard to kill and dangerous to hunt, for they never fear to attack the hunter.

Hunting Matchstick Mushrooms -- The title renders *nameko* (sometimes called the *enoki* [hackberry] mushroom), which grows during the winter on rotted trees. Commercially produced and canned, it belongs to the *matsutake* genus (*Pholita nameko* of the *strophariaceae* class). I invented the word "matchstick mushrooms" to describe these small, slim, and delicate plants.

In the Corridor of Omaezaki Lighthouse -- This lighthouse stands on a promontory some 120 feet above the sea on the southwest corner of Suruga Bay in Shizuoka Prefecture.

Japanese Skies -- Japanese celebrate Boys' Festival on May 5. Swimming carp (*koi*) refer to the *koinobori* -- paper or cloth streamers displayed on poles set up by each family with a male member. Because of their ability to swim upstream against swift currents, carp symbolize courage and perseverance.

Like Music -- "Barque" (or bark) refers to training ships used by the navy and the merchant marine. They have either three or four masts, as well as optional diesel motors. The chip log is the traditional device used to ascertain a sailing vessel's speed.

Living Alone -- An *irori* is a hearth open on all four sides; a spit dangling from the ceiling allows one to hang a kettle over the fire. The hearth universally symbolizes family unity. In Japan it has also been regarded as a sacred spot where the god of fire resides. It is bad luck (and extremely poor manners) to drop anything into the ashes or to put one's feet on the edge board.

Lonely Universe -- Japanese associate singing frogs (*kajika*) -- a small frog indigenous to Japan and the one Maruyama doubtless had in mind -- with summertime. Japanese folklore often depicts frogs as speaking like human beings. As a little boy in Seoul, Maruyama may also have heard the old servant who told him folk tales relate the Korean story that describes frogs as symbols of regret.

Lovely Notion -- "Pond" registers *numa*, in this case a deep, spring-fed pool now a good deal smaller than when the poet lived in Iwanezawa. "Going deep into the woods" consisted of a short jaunt just over the hill from Maruyama's room.

Magical Country -- The title renders *Senkyô*, where hermits abide, a "pure" land far separated from the secular world. Japanese folklore treats such locations as enchanted or "magical" because of the extraordinary events that can occur in places uncorrupted by the stresses of daily life. The *akebi*, a deciduous bush thriving in mountainous areas, has faint red or purple flowers shaped like five-pointed stars; they bloom in April and produce an edible, banana-shaped fruit that matures in autumn. *Shimeji* is an edible mushroom; *maitake* (literally "dancing mushroom") is an edible shelf fungus; *yamadori* are tasty, edible mushrooms growing primarily in beech groves For "matchstick mushrooms," see the note on the poem "Hunting Matchstick Mushrooms."

Man Who Encountered a Bear -- One of Maruyama's favorite poems. He told me he once heard about a man who had confronted a bear somewhat in the manner described in this poem. The source of his information could have been the novelist Ibuse Masuji (b. 1899), who in 1937 published in *Shiki [Four Seasons]* a poem about a bear sliding down a mountain.

Minato Ward, Nagoya -- "Minato" means port or harbor. The Isé Bay Typhoon (October 1959) had caused tidal waves along the immediate seashore, devastating the area and taking many lives. The *Yomiuri Newspaper* asked Maruyama to write a poem about this event. At that time, Maruyama had still not regained his health following an operation for intestinal blockage (despite having been discharged from the hospital on 28 July 1958, more than a year earlier). He agreed to write the poem as long as he did not have to go to Nagoya to view the disaster area.

Mortified Figure -- A photograph of a soldier killed in the Third Arab–Israeli War (5–10 June 1967) stimulated this poem. The poet believed that any publicly viewed or photographed corpse should be "beautified" the way American morticians prepare bodies for viewing. His widow followed the poet's wishes by personally preparing his body for cremation. A close relative helped her transfer the corpse into the coffin, which she then nailed shut so that no one could view his remains.

Mother's Umbrella -- The umbrella symbolizes togetherness. An umbrella with a boy's and a girl's name under it (a common graffito in Japan) functions much like "John loves Jane."

News from the Cape -- Maruyama had never gone diving or snorkeling, much less harpoon fishing.

Night Trees -- Subtitled "For Recitation." The *hinoki* is a type of Japanese cypress; Maruyama also refers to the cypresses that appear in pictures Vincent Van Gogh (1853–1890) painted at Saint Rémy (1889–90). "Aspera" renders the Japanese *muku no ki* (*Aphananthe aspera*), for which I can locate no English equivalent. A *yukata* is a light cotton kimono–like garment used as pajamas by either men or women.

Perversity -- Renders the word *amanojaku*, which means a cross-grained, cranky individual who willfully behaves in a way opposite of what society expects, desires, or requires.

Poet's Words -- Despite his idiosyncratic style, critics usually regard Nakahara Chûya (1907–1937) as a *Shiki [Four Seasons]* poet. He was one of Maruyama's most congenial drinking partners before he died suddenly of acute meningitis. Nakahara was known also as a translator of French poetry, particularly the works of Arthur Rimbaud.

School from Afar -- Deals with Maruyama's recollections of the Third Higher School in Kyoto. In prewar days, such schools functioned as a kind of preparatory course for the university; these higher schools (*kôtô gakkô*) correlate with the German *Gymnasium*. The poet attended this school from 1921 to 1926 when he was between twenty-two and twenty-seven. He wrote the poem in 1939, about a dozen years later.

Snares -- Originally titled, "SEXE *ni tsuite* [On Sex]," this work first appeared in *Shiki [The Four Seasons]* (April 1947). Although the poet's choice of the hyena may be coincidental, note the mythological belief that a female hyena can turn into a male after she mates.

Snowy Field -- Maruyama has doubtless confused the *wappa* with the *wakka*. A *wappa* consists of a wire noose attached to stakes sunk into the side of trails that rabbits follow through the snow. Maruyama describes rather the *wakka*, a hand-launched hoop made of bamboo fashioned into a circle about a foot in diameter. A piece of black cloth fitted over the frame causes a wooshing noise as the *wakka* travels through the air. This presumably sounds to the rabbit like a diving hawk or a kite.

Stars -- Subtitled "For Recitation." See also the note for "High Village." The work in question is *"Les Etoiles."* Alphonse Daudet (1840–1897) began his career with a volume of poetry but gained fame in Paris for his naturalistic tales of life in the city and the provinces. Many featured his own childhood experiences. In interviews, Maruyama expressed special interest in Daudet's depressed boyhood and brief career as a teacher, both of which the poet could identify with.

Strolling the Dunes -- Subtitled "The Dunes at Nakatajima [Island] (I)." Nakata Island lies just off the mouth of the Tenryû River, directly south of Hamamatsu in Shizuoka Prefecture.

That Fellow Within -- This November 1956 poem relates to the aftermath of major surgery in January when doctors removed two-thirds of the poet's ulcerated stomach. Nine days after the operation, a doctor showed him what he had cut out. Since that eerie experience, Maruyama claimed he has had the impression that his body and mind exist unrelated to one another.

Tranquil Festival -- *Mochi*, glutinous rice, is a New Year delicacy made by pounding cooked rice into a sticky mass. *Mochi* ends up in soups, roasted, used as a basis for sweets, and the like. "Spirit" renders *kamisama* (see notes on "The God Who Wept" for the meaning of *kami*).

Working Girl -- People of Iwanezawa tell me they do not recollect that a "factory at the end of the slope" ever existed.

Publication Data on the Collections
From the *Works [Maruyama Kaoru Zenshû]*

Volume V, pages 531-532

1. *Sail–Lamp–Gull [Ho–Ranpu–Kamome]*
   Daiichi Shobô, 5 December 1932

2. *Funeral of the Crane [Tsuru no Sôshiki]*
   Daiichi Shobô, 5 May 1935

3. *Infancy [Yônen]*
   Shiki Sha, 15 June 1935

4. *A Single Day [Ichinichishû]*
   Hangasô, 15 September 1936

5. *Concrete Images [Busshô Shishû]*
   Kawade Shobô, 10 February 1941

6. *The God Who Wept [Namida shita Kami]*
   Usui Shobô, 25 February 1942

7. *Hear the Ship's Bell [Tenshô naru Tokoro]*
   Ooka Sha, 20 September 1943

* *Strong Japan [Tsuyoi Nippon]*
   Kokumin Tosho Kankôkai, 20 October 1944

8. *North Country [Kitaguni]*
   Usui Shobô, 9 September 1946

9. *Magical Country [Senkyô]*
   Sapporo Seiji Sha, 31 March 1948

10. *The Blue Chalkboard [Aoi Kokuban]*
    Nyûfurendo Sha, 10 May 1948

11. *Flowercore [Hana no Shin]*
    Sôgen Sha, 20 June 1948

12. *Lost Youth [Seishun Fuzai]*
    Sôgen Sha, 15 August 1952

13. *The Hostage Sea [Tsuresarareta Umi]*
    Chôryû Sha, 20 November 1962

14. *Moon Passage [Tsuki Wataru]*
    Chôryû Sha, 1 September 1972

15. *Face with Ants [Ari no iru Kao]*
    Chûô Kôron Sha, 30 May 1973

* Maruyama refused to acknowledge *Strong Japan*.

N O T E -- Maruyama chose to include exactly thirty-four poems in his first and seventh collections, the same number selected for *Strong Japan*. His eleventh collection contains forty-three poems (thirty four backward). His last two collections amount to thirty-four poems, plus a long prose passage. The number thirty four derives from the name of the poet's wife, Miyoko. The three Chinese graphs for her name are "3," "4" (born on the fourth of March, the third month), and "*ko*" (the common feminine suffix). Predictably, Maruyama never mentioned to Miyoko this subtle way of honoring her.

Index of English Titles

The source of the poem follows each entry. Roman numerals refer to the volume of *Maruyama Kaoru Zenshû* [Works], published in Tokyo by Kadokawa Shoten (1976-77); Arabic numbers refer to pages in that volume.

Parentheses enclose the month and the year of the first known date of publication; inclusion of a day indicates that the piece first appeared in a newspaper. The date for poems that first appeared in a collection is the date the collection appeared.

Following the # is the number of the collection in which the poem was published; absence of such a number indicates that the poem never appeared in a collection. "Data on the Collections" (p. 117) offers the titles and publication dates corresponding with these numbers.

ABALONE, II:382, (7.21.1970), #14	102
AFTERNOON, I:160 (8.1935), #4	40
APPLES, I:340 (9.1943), #7	54
AUTUMN DREAMS, II:425 (10.1957), #15	92
BELL SONG, I:184 (7.1936), #4	40
BLOSSOMS IN SOUTHERN SEAS, I:314 (5.4.1942), #7	52
BLUE CHALKBOARD, THE, II:14 (11.1946), #10	59
BUTTERFLIES OR BIRDS, I:488 (8.1947), #9	65
BY A POND, II:232 (11.1948), #12	78
BY TRAIN, I:125 (6:1927), #3	36

CAROSSA AND RILKE, II:117 (8.1948), #11	75
CLASS LOG, III:176 (10.1947)	66
CORAL SEA, THE, II:318 (10.1957), #13	91
CRANE, A, III:303 (12.1955)	87
CROW FLOCK, II:238 (4.1950), #12	79
DARK, THE, II:450 (9.1940)	45
DAY–LONG DREAMS, I:151 (1.1935), #4	39
DAZZLING SPRING, I:256 (2.1942), #6	51
DEPRESSING SCENE, I:206 (1.1940), #5	44
DESTITUTE FRIEND, A, II:448 (1.1943)	52
DEVASTATION, II:140 (4.1947), #11	64
DREAMS I SEE IN THE SEA, II:349 (2.1970), #14	102
EVENING MIST, II:175 (6.1948), #11	73
FABRICATIONS, I:114 (12.1926), #3	35
FACE WITH ANTS, II:409 (12.1965), #15	95
FEET OF SAILORS, THE, I:297 (11.1941), #7	49
FISHERMAN, THE, I:117 (12.1926), #3	35
FLAME, II:308 (5.1949), #12	78
FLOWERCORE, II:99 (11.1947), #11	66
FOX FIRE, II:177 (6.1948), #8	74
FUNERAL OF THE CRANE, I:98 (2.1934), #2	38
GOD WHO WEPT, THE, I:210 (12.03.1937), #5	41
GOLDEN CUB, II:385 (4.1972), #14	104
GREENFINCH, II:236 (8.1948), #12	76
GUN EMPLACEMENT, I:28 (1.1931), #1	37
HELM, I:295 (9.1943), #7	53
HIGH VILLAGE, I:408 (7.1946), #8	56
HORIZON, II:374 (7.1963), #14	88
HORSE AT DAWN, I:262 (3.1941), #6	48
HOSTAGE SEA, THE -- On Ocean Day, II:323 (7.20.1956), #13	89

HUNTERS AND I, THE, II:390 (8.1968), #14	99
HUNTING MATCHSTICK MUSHROOMS, I:436 (4.1947), #9	64
ILLUSION IN THE REEF, II:322 (9.1962), #13	94
INFANCY, I:120 (1.1927), #3	36
IN THE CORRIDOR OF OMAEZAKI, II:370 (10.1964), #14	95
INTO CLOUDS ON THE HILL, I:220 (4.1940), #5	45
INTO THE FUTURE, I:264 (1.1941), #6	45
JAPANESE SKIES, THE, I:194 (2.1941), #5	46
JOYS OF SNOW, THE, I:248 (2.1939), #5	42
LIKE A LAMP, II:119 (8.1948), #11	75
LIKE MUSIC, I:285 (6.1941), #7	49
LIVING ALONE, I:391 (7.1946), #8	55
LIVING IN REMOTE MOUNTAINS, I:441 (1.1947), #9	61
LONELY UNIVERSE, THE, II:130 (11.1947), #11	67
LOVELY NOTION, A, I:424 (9.1946), #8	59
LUNAR CALENDAR, THE, I:455 (12.1947), #9	67
MAGICAL COUNTRY, I:433 (1.1947), #9	59
MAN WHO ENCOUNTERED A BEAR, THE, II:396 (1.1954), #14	86
MIDNIGHT MIRROR, III:239 (3.1953)	84
MINATO WARD, NAGOYA, II:423 (10.12.1959), #15	94
MONK HILL, I:122 (6.1935), #3	39
MORTIFIED FIGURE, A, II:411 (9.1967), #15	96
MOTHER'S UMBRELLA, I:443 (1.1947), #9	62
MOUNTAIN PASS, I:86 (9.1934), #2	38
MUD–COLORED PAINTING, I:212 (2.1941), #5	48
NEWS FROM THE CAPE, II:304 (7.27.1950), #12	80
NIGHT JOURNEY, II:208 (4.1949), #12	79
NIGHT TREES, II:259 (4.1951), #12	81
NORTH COUNTRY, I:395 (9.1946), #8	58
OLD POETRY COLLECTION, I:198 (2.1941), #5	47

ON A MOUNTAIN PATH, II:172 (5.1948), #11	73
PERVERSITY, I:238 (2.1936), #5	40
POETRY, III:343 (1.5.1958)	93
POET'S WORDS, A, I:309 (1.1942), #7	50
RIVER, THE, II:431 (1.13.1968), #15	98
SCHOOL FROM AFAR, I:196 (11.1939), #5	43
SEA BEAST, II:331 (9.1956), #13	89
SEA OF OKHOTSK, THE, II:334 (9.1953), #13	85
SELF–RIGHTING LAMP, I:244 (10.1936), #5	41
SNARES, II:399 (4.1972), #14	104
SNOWY FIELD, II:154 (6.1948), #11	72
SONG OF THE GULL, I:19 (12.1931), #1	38
SONG OF THE LAMP, I:18 (12.1931), #1	38
SONG OF THE SAIL, I:17 (12.1931), #1	37
SONG OF THE SPRING BIRD, I:165 (4.1935), #4	39
STARRY NIGHT, II:481 (12.1939)	43
STARS, II:262 (4.1951), #12	82
STREAM, THE -- The Tale of an Old Hunter, II:429 (8.1968), #15	101
STROLLING THE DUNES, II:366 (9.1972), #14	105
SUCH SCENES . . . , II:364 (1.6.1968), #14	97
TELEPHONE POLE, II:74 (5.1948), #10	71
TENTH FLOOR BAR IN THE "Q" HOTEL, II:437 (5.1966), #15	96
THAT FELLOW WITHIN, III:319 (11.1956)	90
THEMES, I:380 (5.1946), #8	54
TOUCHING YOUR TOMBSTONE, I:228 (10.1938), #5	42
TRANQUIL FESTIVAL, I:378 (9.1946), #8	56
TREE IN ME, THE, III:315 (6.1956)	88
TSURUBÉ, I:461 (1.1947), #9,	63
UNFAMILIAR LOCALE, II:230 (11.1948), #12	77
UNSPOKEN LOVE, II:121 (8.1948), #11	76

VIEWS OF THE HARBOR, I:127 (6.1927), #3	36
VISION, II:327 (10.1957), #13	91
WATERFOWL, II:433 (2.3.1968), #15	98
WAVES, I:290 (9.1943), #7	52
WHITE MAGNOLIAS ON MY MIND, III:471 (6.1974)	106
WHITE PICTURES, I:393 (9.1946), #8	57
WITH BUT A FEW WORDS, II:306 (8.1952), #12	83
WORKING GIRL, II:65 (5.1948), #10	71

Former elementary and secondary school teacher, and one-time chief translator and senior editor in Tokyo on the now defunct *Journal of Social and Political Ideas in Japan*, Robert Epp now concentrates on studying and rendering the works of modern Japanese poets. His translation of *Treelike: The Poetry of Kinoshita Yûji* appeared as #4 in Asian Poetry in Translation: Japan.